THE BEGINNINGS
OF CHRISTIAN
THEOLOGY

THE BEGINNINGS
OF
CHRISTIAN
THEOLOGY

BY

J. K. MOZLEY, D.D.
Canon of St Paul's

CAMBRIDGE
AT THE UNIVERSITY PRESS
1931

CAMBRIDGE
UNIVERSITY PRESS

University Printing House, Cambridge CB2 8BS, United Kingdom

Cambridge University Press is part of the University of Cambridge.

It furthers the University's mission by disseminating knowledge in the pursuit of
education, learning and research at the highest international levels of excellence.

www.cambridge.org
Information on this title: www.cambridge.org/9781316619902

© Cambridge University Press 1931

First published 1931
First paperback edition 2016

A catalogue record for this publication is available from the British Library

ISBN 978-1-316-61990-2 Paperback

To

MY WIFE
for all that this book owes
to her and for all that
I owe besides

CONTENTS

PREFACE . . . . *page* ix

Chapter I

THE NEW TESTAMENT BACKGROUND .   I

Chapter II

THE CHRISTIAN FAITH IN THE EARLY
   SECOND CENTURY 19

Chapter III

IN DEFENCE OF THE FAITH . . . 38

Chapter IV

NECESSARY CONTROVERSY AND CON-
   STRUCTIVE THEOLOGY . . . 56

Chapter V

DIFFICULT QUESTIONS AND ATTEMPTS
   TO ANSWER THEM 73

Chapter VI

THE CHRISTIAN PHILOSOPHY OF ALEX-
   ANDRIA 90

Chapter VII

SCRIPTURE, CREED, AND CHURCH . 106

Chapter VIII

THE COUNCIL OF NICAEA . . . 122

PREFACE

This book consists of eight talks, given by invitation of the British Broadcasting Corporation on Sundays during August and September 1930. I have tried to vary the form of the addresses as little as possible in preparing them for the press. The simple and condensed statement which is necessary in speaking to an unseen audience for a limited period of time may, I hope, still be retained with some advantage. The history of Early Christian Doctrine is a subject which presents abundant opportunities for the most minute treatment. It is a field in which a great scholar will be well content to spend a lifetime of exploration. But it is, I am convinced, a great and serious mistake to suppose that it is a field which Christian people, who do not claim or desire to be professional scholars, can afford to leave entirely alone, or that they will find little in it to interest them. On the contrary, I believe that some knowledge of the main stream of Christian theology in the first few centuries is of real importance in connexion with the religious problems and questions of today; and I am sure that the student of the theological movements of those centuries need not find his work dull.

If anyone, after reading this book, should feel the need and wish to supplement it by turning to larger and more adequate volumes, in which much is contained for which no place could here be found, I shall be yet more grateful to the B.B.C. for its invitation, and to the Cambridge University Press for its publication of the results of that invitation.

J. K. MOZLEY

St Augustine's House
Reading
30th October, 1930

CHAPTER I

The New Testament Background

The lectures which are now brought together in this book deal with the broad lines of the development of Christian thinking during a period of nearly three hundred years. They will avoid those side-tracks which afford to the technical scholar fascinating avenues for exploration, but may be confusing to those who are travelling, perhaps for the first time, through this particular region. I shall try also to avoid controversy, although it is not possible to treat such a subject as this without any presuppositions. Christianity, like every philosophy which provides guidance for life and affects man not only on the intellectual side of his nature but through and through, can never be regarded as a branch of archaeology. The greatest scholars approach the study of its history, its institutions, its ethics, and its theology with some kind of attitude of approval or disapproval, of attraction to it or reaction against it. That is the result, partly of the manner of their acquaintance with it, and partly of the view which they take of the world and of life as a whole. But where the impartiality of great scholarship shows itself is in the presentation of facts as truly, as objectively, as possible. Differences of opinion will still remain as to the meaning and the interpretation of the facts, but those opinions should be based on knowledge, as clear and certain as may be, of the facts as they happened, and of the reasons why they happened in the way they did.

And the first business of anyone who speaks or writes on such a subject is to give the facts, not to argue a case. So he may hope, if not entirely to eliminate, yet largely to reduce, the element of controversy.

In this book I am endeavouring to give a survey of Christian theology during a particular period. The history of the growth of the Christian Church and of its relations with the Roman Empire, of the nature and development of its institutions, will be left on one side, and touched on only where that is necessary in the interests of clearness. There is a sufficient reason for this concentration on the theology. I know that the word theology is not a very popular one. It is not at all uncommon to find 'theology' contrasted, very much to its disadvantage, with 'religion'. But, after all, theology stands simply for that ordered thinking about God and man and the world and the relations between them which is implicit, and necessarily tends to become more explicit, in all religion. In the most primitive form of worship a theology was latent. Man has an unquenchable desire to understand the scheme of things in which he finds himself. It is this intellectual curiosity, which, from the psychological standpoint, underlies theology. What, I think, some people fear, is a divorce of theology from life. I will not say that theology has never been presented to them in such a form as to make such a fear justifiable. But a wider knowledge of any theology, and a deeper penetration to its roots, would show that any such detachment from life has indicated a debasement of theology and is no mark of its true nature. One of the means of correcting such a misunderstanding is a study of the history of theology. That is certainly the case with regard to Christianity. By means of the history we come to know, not vaguely, but with that definiteness which belongs to all true historical knowledge, what the doctrines involved in the theology are, and how they attained the forms in which they have come down to us.

At the outset, I must give some account of the background of all later Christian thinking. It is in that light (not the only possible light) in which I wish to regard the New Testament. For, apart from the New Testament, the subsequent theological developments cannot be understood. So we must try to appreciate the general character of the New Testament and especially those features of it which have special relevance to later movements of Christian thought.

From the first, one fact needs to be realized. For the early Christians, about the middle of the first century of our era, when the New Testament books began to be composed and to be read in different Christian communities, there was one and only one collection of sacred books. That was the Old Testament. And it prejudges in no way the question of inspiration if one says that the writers of the books of our New Testament had no idea or intention of compiling what we may call a second volume of sacred books. The notion of a New Testament alongside of the Old Testament was in no way, as far as we can see, in the mind of the writers. This is not unimportant. If the New Testament had been deliberately compiled as sacred literature or as a manual or text-book of doctrine, I think we should be very naturally surprised both by some of the things it contains and by the fact that there are other things which it does not contain. The key to the understanding of what is in the New Testament and of what is not is to be found in the right attitude to the New Testament as literature.

But before any discussion of the character of this literature, there is a previous question to be asked and answered. How did it come about that this literature was ever written? The answer to this question may not tell us anything about the particular and special circumstances under which the various books were written, and yet may explain the literature as a whole. Such an answer is forthcoming: the literature itself is grounded in, and grows out of, a theology. The New Testament which is the background of later Christian theology has its own background in an already existing Christian theology, that is, in a teaching about Christ already proclaimed and accepted. Two references will make this plain. First, consider what St Paul says in the opening verses of the fifteenth chapter of the first Epistle to the Corinthians, which form the prelude to the long statement and argument about the resurrection. I take Dr Moffatt's translation:

Now, brothers, I would have you know the Gospel I once preached to you, the Gospel you received, the Gospel in which you have your footing, the Gospel by which you are saved—provided you adhere to my statement of it—unless indeed your faith was all haphazard.

St Paul then goes on to tell his readers how he 'passed on' to them what he had himself 'received'—Christ's death 'for our sins', His burial, and His resurrection

4

on the third day. It is obvious that while special circumstances caused him to write to the Corinthians when he did, and on the various subjects which find a place in the letter, he would never have written to them at all, had they not been persons to whom he had once preached the Gospel and who had received as true that Gospel when he preached it, and had he not himself at an earlier time ceased to be simply Saul of Tarsus and become instead Paul an Apostle of Jesus Christ. This first Epistle to the Corinthians has, therefore, behind it, and presupposes, a Gospel or good news about Christ. And while it is true that a distinction may be drawn between the good news and a theology, the distinction is only relative and provisional. This good news inevitably involves and expresses itself in a theology, in ordered notions about God and the world and men, with which the good news about Christ is most intimately related.

The second reference is to a passage which occurs in the preface to Bishop Westcott's book *The Gospel of the Resurrection*. In it that great teacher was concerned to state what he held to be of the very essence of Christianity in respect of the personal attitude to Christ. He says:

the earliest known description of a Christian is 'one who *believes on Christ*, and not one who *believes Christ*'. Or, in other words, a Christian is essentially one who throws himself with absolute trust upon a living Lord, and not simply one who endeavours to obey the commands and follow the example of a dead Teacher.

It was this attitude to Christ which explains the existence of the literature of the New Testament. People sometimes speak as though the substance of Christianity were to be found in the Sermon on the Mount, and Christian discipleship meant trying to live up to the level of the revelation of the moral ideal given in the Sermon. Now, as to the relative importance of different elements in Christianity, or as to what constitutes the essence of Christianity, there are differences of opinion; but I would claim that it is not a mere opinion, but a practical certainty, that we should never have known anything about the Sermon on the Mount, or about the Jesus who in that Sermon spoke words of such amazing moral beauty and power, unless the first Christians had been men and women who, in Westcott's words, believed on Christ, and trusted Him absolutely as the living Lord who by His resurrection had overcome death. It was in that faith and trust that Christianity and Christians were born and nurtured. Apart from it we have no reason to suppose that there would have been a Christian religion, or that a literature would have come into existence to make known to subsequent ages the existence of a great Jewish moral teacher, called Jesus, who had been put to death by order of a Roman Governor. But from within a community, scattered in different parts of the Roman Empire, which believed that Jesus had risen from the dead, and was convinced thereby of the unique and unparalleled importance of His Person, came the books which we know as the New Testament.

When this fact is overlooked there is a danger lest all that we owe to modern scholarship for the light it has thrown on various problems connected with the New Testament books may result in our failing to see the wood for the trees. The wealth of information on all sorts of points of not unimportant detail can obscure what still remain the simple lines of this literature in regard both to origin and object. Origin and object and the union between them are discernible within the New Testament in the words which the author of the fourth Gospel uses at the end of the twentieth chapter of his book. St John is explaining the selection he has made out of a much larger material of 'signs'—to use his own word—wrought by Jesus, and this is what he says:

These were written that ye might believe that Jesus is the Christ, the Son of God, and that believing ye might have life in his name.

But that motive was no personal idiosyncrasy of St John's. In one way or another, *faith*, actual or to be awakened, in Jesus as the Christ, the Son of God, was the bond uniting the writers of the New Testament books and those for whom they wrote.

It is in this that the unity of the New Testament is manifested. Here are these twenty-seven books, in many ways very diverse: diverse in authorship, in place and occasion of writing, diverse in type and quality of writing. Yet this assemblage, this little library of books, is not a casual collection, united by the fact of being bound up between two covers. There is an internal unity, a unity in the books reflecting a unity existing prior to the books. That unity is not to be understood except in relation to its centre, Jesus Christ. Great historical personalities are sometimes, though not always, forces making for some kind of deeper unity and becoming themselves the centres of

7

unifying movements extending outwards into one or more departments of human life and thought. If we look for instances in the ancient world, we shall find them among the Hebrews in Moses and David; in Greece in Socrates, both in what he essentially was and in what he became as interpreted by Plato; also in Alexander the Great; in Rome in Julius Caesar. What is true of them is true also, in this respect, of Jesus Christ. He meant the appearance of a new centre of unity. Those who 'believed on Him' found that to be so from the first. Statements expressing that unity, making its rational grounds clear, and tracing out its consequences, abound in the New Testament. There is an atmosphere of freshness and wonder, the sense of an entry into a world of truth and power in which 'old things have passed away: nay, they have become new', and the dweller in this world is himself a new creation. This atmosphere is one of the most remarkable features of these books. There is no single word more truly descriptive of primitive Christianity than the word 'Gospel'. Christianity *was* Gospel, that is good news. It was good news for men because it was good news about God and His Kingdom. And it was good news, not in the way in which a philosophy might be good news as throwing light upon the mysteries of existence through the processes of human discovery and reflexion. The stress did not fall upon that side of the matter, though obviously that side has always to be taken into account. But the stress fell on the movement from God to the world, on what God had given and done in His love. This is what the New Testament writers have in mind when they speak so often of 'grace'. This is why there is so deep a spirit of gratitude revealed in what they write. It is the explanation of certain sharp turns of thought as when St Paul says 'but now having known God', and immediately corrects himself with 'or rather having been known by God'. It is the background of phrases which cause not a little difficulty when they are taken and interpreted by themselves, and not viewed in the light of their whole context, as when St Peter addresses his Christian readers as 'elect according to the foreknowledge of God'.

Now, when the first Christians, and, later in the first century, the New Testament writers thought of God's gifts and grace and used the phrase 'the Gospel', they thought also and necessarily of Jesus. The good news came through Jesus: but, more than that: to arrive at the full weight of primitive Christian thinking one must say that the good news was Jesus: He was not on the circumference of their thoughts as a witness or herald or prophet of good news might be; He was at the centre of their thinking, because for them He was at the centre of the good news. The titles used of Jesus in their thinking about Him make this central position of Jesus plain. There is room for different opinions among scholars as to the exact implications of these titles and as to the way in which they came to be attached to Jesus, but not one of them would have been used of Him, unless it had been believed that He was the centre of religion in a way in which neither Moses nor any of the great prophets of Israel was central. He was the Christ, that is the Messiah on whose coming pious Israelites had set their hopes; the Servant of the Lord, that is the suffering Servant whose vocation and destiny to bear the sins of others was written in the fifty-third chapter of Isaiah; the beloved and only Son of God; the Lord. This last title, whatever its origin, could not fail to recall to Greek-speaking believers, who knew the Old Testament in the Greek version, the phrase ὁ Κύριος 'the Lord' used in that version as the translation of the sacred personal name of the God of Israel—Jehovah or Jahweh. All this may be regarded as bearing witness, in the first place, to primitive Christian thought about Jesus and not to what scholars have called the self-consciousness of Jesus, that is to what Jesus thought about Himself; yet there is abundant ground for the belief that those titles, either actually or implicitly, go back to Jesus Himself, and truly represent His mind, so that in using these titles of Him the primitive Christian community and the New Testament writers were not striking out a new line.

It is this fact which makes any search for a religion in the New Testament, which shall avoid theology, so unprofitable and so certainly doomed to failure. It is not the question of the presence or absence of technical terms or of something in the nature of a creed. Such terms are to be found, and the confession 'Jesus is Lord' is of the nature of a creed. But underlying that is the fact that in the New Testament Jesus is not so much the Teacher of religion as the object of religion. For that reason, any detachment of the Gospels from the rest of the New Testament is an unscientific procedure and likely to lead to a misunderstanding of the Gospels themselves. No books, and I am thinking especially of the first three Gospels, have ever been subjected to such close examination as during the last century has been the case with these. And out of the agreements and disagreements of scholars who have devoted themselves to this work, one thing, at least, stands out clearly: the Gospels have as their one true context, necessary to the understanding of them, the life and faith of the early Christian communities. It is, of course, impossible to change the order in which the books stand in any edition of the New Testament which would gain official sanction and meet with general approval. But it must always be remembered that, broadly speaking, the Epistles were written before the Gospels. Therefore, if, in serious study of the New Testament, the student would begin with one or more of the Epistles and then go on to a Gospel, he would gain an invaluable background and would be approaching the reading of the Gospel from the same angle as the author who wrote it.

There is, then, this unity centred in a Person discernible in the New Testament, a unity to which we shall rightly attach the adjectives 'religious' and 'theological'. But it is an inclusive unity, and variety of presentation and difference of emphasis are to be found within it: and of this a little more needs to be said.

Many will be familiar with what are called the symbols of the evangelists, that is with the four living creatures who in Christian art are severally associated with the Gospel writers. The symbol of St Matthew is a man, of St Mark a lion, of St Luke a calf, of St John an eagle. It would be rather pedantic to try to find precise relation between each symbol and the character of the evangelist and of the Gospel in question. Yet in two cases, at least, the appropriateness is striking. The lion is the symbol of power, and in St Mark's Gospel the power of Jesus is continually noticeable. We cannot overlook the power of His personality working upon people and through events. There is a special quality attaching to the actions of Jesus even more than to His words of which we are conscious in reading this Gospel, and it is a fair inference that it was on this that the evangelist wished to lay stress for the benefit of his readers. The eagle is the symbol of heaven-ward movement, and none could more appropriately represent the work of the fourth evangelist as he seeks to show what Jesus meant to God and God to Jesus in the mystery of divine Fatherhood and Sonship. In the rest of the New Testament there is a similar diversity to be recognized. Jesus is at the centre of the picture, but not always in the same way. Take such letters as 1 Thessalonians, Romans, Colossians, and the Epistle to the Hebrews, and add the Revelation of St John. The pictures there painted, if I may continue the metaphor, are obviously different pictures, but they are clearly of the same Person, and, I would add, they do not clash with one another. To primitive Christian thought, as illustrated in divers portions and in divers manners, if I may adapt to this purpose the beginning of the Epistle to the Hebrews, Jesus Christ could be the one who should come to gather His people to Himself; the second Adam, head of a new race; the ground and goal of the whole process of creation; the divine priest and sacrifice, fulfilling the old sacrificial system; and the Lamb in the midst of the host of heaven, receiving the praises of those whom He had redeemed.

Now it is clear that this diversity of portraiture, which, conceived of intellectually, is a diversity of interpretation, amounts to a number of ways of describing the significance and the greatness of Jesus: and these descriptions involve ideas which certainly would be very unfitting and would, indeed, be impossible in the case of one who was thought of as being, in the last resort, simply a supremely good man or a supremely great prophet. At the same time (and this needs always to be borne in mind, both for its own sake, and in relation to later developments) the New Testament writers had no doubt at all as to the real humanity of Jesus Christ. That is as plainly shown in the fourth Gospel as in the second, and receives its most remarkable expression in the Epistle to the Hebrews. There are particular difficulties in connexion with this letter to the Hebrews, and a point of approach to the meaning of Christianity not, at first sight, very congenial to some modern ideas, which causes it to be in all probability one of the least well-known parts of the New Testament. This is the more unfortunate because in at least two lines of thought the writer develops an argument which, so far from being out of touch with our modern outlook, is in striking harmony with it. For, first of all, if we penetrate to the heart of what he says about the temporary and incomplete character of the old Jewish priesthood and sacrifice we see in his words the unfolding of that principle of progressive revelation which must be grasped by whoever wishes to understand the Christian notion of the relation between the Old Testament and the New. About that I must be content with this brief reference. The other matter is of more immediate concern. The writer to the Hebrews was anxious to bring home to his readers the fact that Jesus Christ was the true high priest. Now, the work which the priests did under the Levitical law, and the representative character which they bore, were bound up with the fact that a common humanity united the priests and those worshippers on whose behalf they made intercession and offered sacrifices to God. In other words the reality of priesthood fell within the reality of a common human nature. But what then as to Him whom the author of Hebrews was to depict as the one who fulfilled in what He was and what He did all that true priesthood and sacrifice could ever be? What as to Jesus? Could that bond of a common humanity exist between men and one who was describable as 'the effulgence of God's glory and the very image of His substance, upholding all things by the word of his power'? The writer insists that that bond did exist; it is a truth on which he is specially glad to dwell, one that he feels should be full of encouragement to his readers. I will give some examples of his teaching:

As we have a great high priest, then, who has passed through the heavens, Jesus the Son of God, let us hold fast to our confession; for ours is no high priest who is incapable of sympathising with our weaknesses, but one who has been tempted in every respect like ourselves, yet without sinning.

In the days of his flesh, with bitter cries and tears, he offered prayers and supplications to him who was able to save him from death; and he was heard, because of his godly fear. Thus, Son though he was, he learned by all he suffered how to obey, and by being thus perfected he became the source of eternal salvation for all who obey him.

It will become clear later on that this emphasis upon the true human nature of Christ was of great doctrinal importance in the face of certain strange ideas which, however grotesque and incredible they may appear to us, were put forward and tenaciously held by some religious teachers over a considerable stretch of time. At this point it is sufficient to say that the New Testament knows nothing of a Christianity rooted in attachment to a set of abstract ideas. Its roots are not to be found in anything divorced from actual history, but in a historical Person—Jesus—who lived and died and, so the first Christians believed, did as truly rise from the dead. And that Person was no angel or demigod: Son of God they confessed Him to be, but also really and fully man, one whose human nature was as truly human as that of the men whom He came to help and save.

The facts which have been noted should be sufficient to show that from the standpoint of the New Testament writings, and, therefore, of the Christian attitude to Jesus which they represent, the opposition sometimes suggested as existing between the Jesus of History and the Christ of Faith did not exist. Read the opening chapters of the Acts of the Apostles, and note how the emphasis falls on these two convictions, shared by the first little company of believers and proclaimed at first to Jews, later to all men,—the convictions that Jesus was the Christ and that He had risen from the dead.

There were plenty of problems connected with the Person of Jesus to exercise the minds of Christian thinkers in the centuries which followed the events of His life, but an attachment to Jesus which took no account of His Messiahship or of His resurrection, and found in Him and His life simply the revelation of transcendent human goodness, was never suggested as the true line which thought should follow out in order to reach the truth about Him. Whatever views we may take as to the possibility of such an attitude, it has nothing in common with the New Testament.

The fact that Christian theology during the first three centuries was so largely taken up with the best way of interpreting the Person of Jesus Christ explains the emphasis laid upon the place occupied by Jesus Christ in the New Testament literature. It is with a sense of this convergence of the books upon Jesus Christ that the great outstanding passages which have had special importance in the history of doctrine can best be approached. To the opening of the Epistle to the Hebrews I have already referred; by the side of it I would place the first chapter of the Epistle to the Colossians from the twelfth verse onwards, verses five to eleven of the second chapter of the Epistle to the Philippians, and the Prologue—that is the first eighteen verses—of the fourth Gospel. These are tremendous passages, and no one who reads them thoughtfully can fail to regard them as among the most remarkable (one might go farther and say the most remarkable) things ever written.

Jesus was crucified in the year A.D. 29, to give the most probable date. The Epistle to the Philippians was written about the year 62; almost the same space of time separates those two dates as divides us from the death of Mr Gladstone. The Jesus of History is the Christ of Faith for St Paul; but He had been that for the community of believers before St Paul wrote to Philippi and before St Paul's conversion about the year A.D. 35. Much as all later Christian thought concerning Christ owed to St Paul, it did not owe to him the essential principle of identity, 'Jesus is the Christ, the Son of God'. It was for that fact of identity that Jesus went to the Cross: asked at His trial before the high priest by that foremost figure in the Jewish Church whether He was the Christ, the Son of the Blessed, Jesus said 'I am'. Those two words mark a turning-point in the history of the world.

One further feature of the New Testament background should be noted: Christianity was from the first the faith of a community; Christians were the Church, the *ecclesia*, of God, owing their existence to what Christ, the Son of God, had done for them. They thought of His death in terms of redemption and sacrifice, of what we call atonement. And when they thought of the power whereby the Church was able to bear its witness and do its work, the power which was at the same time a bond of union between the Church and God the Father and the Lord Jesus Christ, they described it as the Spirit, or, more exactly, in a phrase very rare in the Old Testament and very common in the New, the Holy Spirit. The prominence given to the idea of the Holy Spirit is one of the most note-worthy facts in the New Testament literature. Except for the Lord's Prayer there is no passage in the New

Testament so familiar in connexion with the prayers of Christian people as the end of the second Epistle to the Corinthians—'the grace of our Lord Jesus Christ, and the love of God, and the Fellowship of the Holy Spirit be with you all'. There are other places where a similar bringing together of the Father, and the Lord Jesus and the Spirit occurs: I may refer to Romans viii, 9–17, 1 Corinthians xii, 3–6, Ephesians iv, 1–6, 1 St Peter i, 2. Such passages, besides their own intrinsic importance, are signs which point out the character of primitive Christian religion, and point towards the course which Christian theology was to take. To be in the true religious relation to God meant for the Christian a necessary relation to the Lord Jesus and to the Holy Spirit. So, from this beginning, Christian religion handed on the task of ordered and systematic thinking to Christian theology.

CHAPTER II

The Christian Faith in the Early Second Century

In passing from that background of Christian theology which we possess in the New Testament, it may be well to recall two facts about the New Testament books on which I laid stress. One is that these books, Gospels, Acts, Epistles, and Revelation, were not written as a second volume in a sacred library. If we take the literature as a whole we must say that there was no conscious intention of adding a second volume to the Old Testament. The other fact is the concentration in these books upon the Person of Jesus Christ. If we ask what it is that binds them together into a unity, we shall answer 'a common attitude to Jesus Christ'. He is at the centre of this literature, and, therefore, was at the centre of a faith and devotion antecedent to the literature.

Now we cannot be certain of the date when each New Testament book was written. But, broadly speaking, we can say that, with very few possible exceptions, these books were written during the first century of our era, between the years 48 and 100. Again, while one or two early Christian writings besides the books which compose our New Testament are earlier than the year 100, the bulk of these later writings are subsequent to the year 100. So we may regard this round number, the year 100, as more or less precisely dividing the books of the New Testament from other Christian writings. In those writings of which I am now going to speak we shall see that the New Testament attitude to Jesus Christ continues; we see also that the New Testament books are beginning to be regarded as sacred literature, to which appeal can confidently be made. That is, we see the beginnings of the process which led to the formation of what is called the Canon of the New Testament. Of that something will be said in a later chapter. Here it is sufficient to say that the word 'Canon' is taken from the equivalent Greek word of which the simplest translation is 'rule'. The idea of the Canon has been described by a great scholar, Dr Alexander Souter, as that of an 'exclusive selection of sacred books for use in public worship'. Such books had a special authority. They were the work of apostles or of men closely associated with apostles, and they contained the substance of the Christian Faith. References to them became more and more common in the Christian writings of the second century.

These writings are generally grouped together under the title of 'The Apostolic Fathers'. There is a convenient edition of them, with the original Greek text and an English translation facing one another, in the Loeb Library published by Heinemann. The editor is Dr Kirsopp Lake. The phrase 'The Apostolic Fathers' is not altogether satisfactory, but we may use it as indicating that the writers in question stood near to the apostolic age, and may, in one or two instances, have been associated with apostles. The writers and writings are as follows: there is a letter by Clement, who writes in the name of the Roman Church to the Church of Corinth with regard to a case of grave disorder which had taken place in the Corinthian Church. This Clement was, according to early lists of Bishops, the third or fourth Bishop of Rome during the last decades of the first century. His letter was written perhaps a year or two earlier than the year 100. Next comes the Second Epistle of Clement to the Corinthians, of which it has been epigrammatically said that it is not an epistle, and it is not by Clement, but it *is* to the Corinthians. Even this is not certain; it may have had nothing to do with Corinth. What is clear is that it is a sermon preached in some Christian Church. Then come the most famous of all early Christian writings outside the New Testament, namely the Epistles of Ignatius. Ignatius was Bishop of Antioch in Syria. He had been condemned to death, as far as we know, simply for his profession of Christianity. Considerably before the end of the first century the Roman Empire had taken up an attitude of definite hostility to the Christian Church. Christianity had become a form of faith which the Empire did not recognize as lawful. That had now become one great and clear distinction between Christianity and Judaism. It meant a wide change from what had been the case forty or fifty years earlier. The descriptions which we have in the book of the Acts of the Apostles of St Paul's relations with various Roman officials make it quite clear that at that date Christianity was not regarded as in itself a penal offence. The Roman Governor Festus was sure that Paul had done nothing worthy of death and bonds. It was true that Paul held beliefs about Jesus and His resurrection which seemed to Festus very extraordinary, but there was nothing criminal in that.

How it came about that the Empire changed its attitude of toleration into one of hostility, leading to persecution, is a question which to this day has not, I believe, been quite satisfactorily answered. On one or two points connected with it I propose to touch later when dealing with defences of the Christian faith written about the middle of the second century. Here we may be content to note the fact. A Christian was liable to criminal proceedings simply because he bore the name of Christian. This, apparently, had happened in the case of Ignatius. He was tried, and condemned to be thrown to the wild beasts in the arena at Rome. On his way to Rome he wrote seven letters, six to various Christian Churches, and one to Polycarp who was Bishop of Smyrna. Their date cannot be precisely fixed, but the year 115 may be taken as approximate.

We come next to the Epistle of Polycarp to the Philippians. This was written soon after the martyrdom of Ignatius at Rome, and was sent to the Church at Philippi with copies of the letters of Ignatius which Polycarp possessed. Polycarp himself was to suffer martyrdom at Smyrna some forty years later, on February 23rd, 155. He wrote other letters which were known at the end of the second century, but only this one has survived.

The document which follows is one of the most puzzling in early Christian literature. Its title is *Teaching of the Twelve Apostles*: it has a subtitle *Teaching of the Lord to the heathen by the Twelve Apostles.* From the first Greek word, meaning 'teaching', it is always referred to as *The Didaché.* It has been described as 'a manual of Church instruction', and the title shows that the author claimed that it embodied apostolic precepts. But we know neither its author nor its date nor the place where it was written. Its very history is romantic; for while it was known to have existed, it had been lost, and was only discovered in 1875 in a library at Constantinople. It is possible that it was written in Syria, some time in the second century. It is a composite work, and one part of it may be considerably earlier than the rest.

Then comes the Epistle of Barnabas. But, despite its title, there is no claim in the body of the work that it was written by Barnabas, the companion of St Paul, and scholars do not regard it as his. But it is to be dated in the first half of the second century; its main purpose is to insist that the ceremonial law of the Old Testament was never intended to be literally observed; the author has a symbolical method of interpretation which had, indeed, already been employed by the learned Jewish writer, Philo, who, in Alexandria, had come under the influence of Greek philosophy.

Three more documents remain, and form the second volume of the English edition of the Apostolic Fathers in the Loeb Library. First we have a long work called *The Shepherd of Hermas*. This work belongs to what is called apocalyptic literature. It consists of revelations, 'apocalypses', made to a certain Hermas, and one of those who give these revelations is an angel who appears in the guise of a shepherd. Three main parts are to be distinguished—*Visions*, *Commandments*, and *Similitudes*. It may have been written at different times, but the work as a whole belongs to the middle of the second century. About the end of the second century someone connected with the Church of Rome drew up a list of Christian books which were reckoned as authoritative. What he says of this writing of Hermas may be given in full:

The Shepherd was written quite lately in our times by Hermas, while his brother Pius, the bishop, was sitting in the chair of the Church of the City of Rome: and therefore it ought indeed to be read, but it cannot to the end of time be publicly read in the Church to the people, either among the prophets, who are complete in number, or among the Apostles.

Pius was bishop about the year 148, which gives us approximately Hermas' date. Hermas was a member of the Church in Rome, and his book is mainly concerned with Christianity on its ethical side, and, from our point of view, it suffers from the obscurity which attaches to the author's use of symbolism: yet, as we shall see, it has its own theological importance.

It may seem curious to find the writing entitled *The Martyrdom of Polycarp* bound up with the Apostolic Fathers. But we need not quarrel with a practice which has led to so interesting a document being better known than would otherwise have been the case. It is a contemporary account of the death of its bishop sent by the Church of Smyrna to the Church of Philomelium.

Finally we have an anonymous but very striking work called *The Epistle to Diognetus*. It has no particular right to be ranked with a collection to which the general name of the Apostolic Fathers is given. It is more like a formal statement and defence of the nature of the Christian religion than are any of the works which we have hitherto noticed. Moreover, it may belong more closely to the end than to the beginning of the second century. However, its position may for our purposes be accepted; and it certainly throws valuable light on Christian belief.

Now, in using this material we must remember that it was the stress of a particular situation or emergency which gave it birth. Neither the New Testament writings nor the Christian literature of the first half of the second century bear the stamp of a theological text-book. Text-books give us the results of creative thinking rather than that thinking itself. The New Testament is rich in creative thinking; the immediately succeeding literature does not possess this great quality to anything like the same extent. Yet there is still a certain ferment of new ideas, and that is something which we do not easily associate with a text-book. The ideas have not yet been precisely formulated nor have they acquired the property of orderly relation to one another. Moreover, terminology (or exact wording) lagged behind thought. Ideas need to be given adequate clothing or expression; but that does not happen all at once. The Apostolic Fathers were not great constructive thinkers, nor were they exercising themselves in the problem of fixing the right word to the right idea. But I think that for this very reason they are the more instructive. The theology of the Apostolic Fathers is not the theology of the armchair which is always to be suspected, nor of the professor's chair to which we often do well to listen. But in what they say we hear the notes of an ardent faith and of a living experience which point towards a promised land of a rich and

25

harmonious theology, of which, however, they are not able as yet to take possession.

But an uncompleted theology is not necessarily an indefinite theology, and on a number of matters of high importance there were both definiteness of conviction and clarity of expression. Take, for instance, the doctrine of God. The Christian Church was heir to Hebrew Monotheism. It would no more have occurred to one of the New Testament writers or to one of the Apostolic Fathers to have doubted the truth of this tradition than it would have occurred to a Jew steeped in the thought and language of the Prophets of his race. Hermas is not always typical, but here he may speak for all, and this is how he begins the writing of those *Commandments* which in his vision had been revealed to him by the Shepherd.

First of all believe that God is one, who made all things and perfected them, and made all things to be out of that which was not, and contains all things, and is Himself alone uncontained.

Here we have that stress upon the unity of God and upon His relation to the world as its Creator which has always been characteristic of Christian theology. God alone exists in His own right; everything else is dependent upon Him. Neither mind nor matter possesses any independence of Him, except in so far as God has conferred upon created spirits a gift of real freedom. From the first the epithet παντοκράτωρ, that is literally 'all-controlling', was used of God. The Latin translation *omnipotens* and the English 'almighty' are words which need to be used with a certain care. For Christian theology has never meant, when describing God as almighty, that He could do literally anything and everything. It has, for instance, not meant that God could make evil to be good and good evil. Any such idea would make nonsense of the fundamental belief that God, in His own nature, is perfectly good. Nor, again, has it meant that God could make a thing at one and the same time both to exist and not to exist. For such a view would destroy the possibility of any rational thinking about God, and is, in itself, completely unmeaning. But the word 'almighty' means that God can do whatever is possible, whatever is not intrinsically impossible in virtue of such considerations as I have adduced.

In this the Apostolic Fathers followed the New Testament. They also followed the New Testament in holding that the world was very far from what it ought to be, and from what God wished it to be. That was because of the fact of moral evil, which was interpreted as revolt from God and rebellion against His will. The possibility of this rebellion was bound up with the gift of freedom to created spirits. Not only man but other spiritual beings had gone astray from God, they had followed their own desires instead of always seeking to do God's will. One may go farther and say that moral evil meant the perversion of desire as contrasted with the right direction of desire. The early Christian thinkers were not philosophical enquirers into that darkest of all problems, the problem of evil and of its origin. But they held quite firmly that evil was not inevitable, and that it was not a quality of matter as contrasted with spirit. The importance of this we shall see later.

It was this belief that the world had gone astray from God which led to the emphasis upon redemption. The word 'redemption' means literally a 'buying back' and is the equivalent of the Greek word *apolutrosis*. Sometimes attempts were made to interpret this 'buying back' literally rather than metaphorically. Into that, at the moment, I need not go. Suffice it to say that redemption, anyhow, meant deliverance and restoration. And that deliverance was two-fold; there was a present deliverance and a future one. In the present there was a deliverance from the power of evil for Christian believers; in the future, when Christ came again, the world itself would be delivered by being changed. That was the hope of the Kingdom of God, of the new Creation, when, in St Paul's words, the creation itself would be delivered from the bondage of corruption into the glorious liberty of the children of God. This insistence upon the future was very characteristic of early Christian thought. It resulted in strong expression being given to a contrast between an evil present and a blessed future. So, in the homily ascribed to Clement, the preacher says:

Now the world that is, and the world to come are two enemies. This world speaks of adultery, and corruption, and love of money, and deceit, but that world bids these things farewell.

In accordance with this outlook the hope was cherished that the end of this world or age would soon come. 'Let grace come and let this world pass away', says the author of the *Didaché*, and he repeats the two Aramaic words which St Paul had used just at the end of the first Epistle to the Corinthians, *Maran atha*, 'Our

Lord, come'. One of the early second-century writers, Papias, Bishop of Hierapolis in Asia Minor, of whose writings only a few fragments have survived, expressed his hopes for the future in a way which Eusebius the great Church historian, who has been called the Father of Church History, decidedly condemned. Eusebius wrote in the fourth century and refers to Papias as follows: 'He said there would be a certain millennium after the resurrection, and that there would be a bodily reign of Christ on this very earth". Papias, he continues, did not understand the mystic character of passages in the apostolic tradition for he was a man of small intelligence. But it is only fair to Papias to point out that in his interpretation he did not stand alone.

This hope set on the future did not involve any in-attention to a present relation of Jesus Christ to the Christian Church. As to what Christ had done, stress was laid on His work as Teacher and as Saviour. As Teacher He was the One from whom men could gain the true knowledge of God and a higher law of life. Thus, in the *Didaché*, the following form of thanksgiving is to be used after the reception of the Lord's Supper, or, as the writer calls it, the Eucharist: 'We give thanks to Thee, O Holy Father, for Thy Holy Name which Thou didst make to tabernacle in our hearts, and for the knowledge and faith and immortality which Thou didst make known to us through Jesus Thy Child'. And Hermas hands on the teaching given him by the Shepherd, that the Son of God showed the people the 'ways of life, and gave them the law which He "received from His Father"'. This knowledge followed after the cleansing of the people's sins, and Hermas thus connects the teaching and the saving work of Christ. Clement in his letter emphasizes both the need for repentance and the blessing of forgiveness, and associates both with the work of Christ, and especially with His death. In one striking passage he says 'let us fix our gaze on the blood of Christ, and let us know that it is precious to His Father, because it was poured out for our salvation, and brought the grace of repentance to all the world'. Ignatius often expresses himself in terms of fervent gratitude and love to Christ for what He had done. 'My spirit', he tells the Ephesians, 'is devoted to the Cross, which is an offence to unbelievers, but to us salvation and eternal life.' And writing to the Philadelphians he describes the charters, that is, the foundation facts, as 'Jesus Christ—His cross, and death, and resurrection, and the faith which is through Him'. Again Barnabas lays stress on the death of Christ; 'for it was for this reason that the Lord endured to deliver up His flesh to corruption, that we should be sanctified by the remission of sin, that is, by His sprinkled blood'. In language of this kind we have not reached a precisely formulated theory. But we see the working of the belief that the death of Christ was the true sacrifice for sin, and the influence of the fifty-third chapter of Isaiah with its portrait of the Servant of the Lord who suffered for the sins of others. This sense of redemption and forgiveness, as of blessings to be enjoyed in the present age, needs to be remembered alongside of the expectation of a new order of things, a 'new heaven and earth' in the future.

It is in connexion with this firm conviction of all the blessings which they owed to Jesus Christ that we can best approach the character of the belief in Jesus Christ which these early Christian writers possessed. And their faith was the faith of the various Christian communities then existing in the world, if we take them as a whole. It is true that the Jewish-Christian, as contrasted with the Gentile-Christian, communities seem to have been content to think of Jesus as the Messiah, and not to have gone beyond that; in particular, they rejected that high estimate of Jesus as the Son of God to which St Paul gave expression in his Epistles. But our information is fragmentary, and, in any case, this type of doctrine did not represent the main stream of Christian thought. That stream carried in its deep waters the conviction of the divinity of Jesus. The homily ascribed to Clement begins with the words 'Brethren, we must think of Jesus Christ as of God, as of the Judge of the living and the dead'. Ignatius, again and again, affirms this doctrine. He addresses the Ephesian Church as 'united and chosen through true suffering by the will of the Father and Jesus Christ our God'. Its members have kindled their brotherly task (he is thinking of their kindness to himself) 'by the blood of God'. When he wrote to the Roman Church he was afraid that representations on his behalf might be made by that Church which would rob him of that martyrdom which he so ardently desired: 'Suffer me', he cries, 'to follow the example of the Passion of my God'. In writing to Smyrna he begins his letter, after the introduction, with the words 'I give glory to Jesus Christ, the God who has thus given you wisdom'. In a number of passages Ignatius speaks of the relation of Christ to the Father. 'Jesus Christ before the ages was with the Father, and at the end of them was made manifest. He came forth from the one Father, and is with one, and departed to one.' 'The divine prophets', he tells the Magnesians, 'lived according to Jesus Christ. Therefore they were also persecuted, being inspired by His grace, to convince the disobedient that there is one God, who manifested Himself through Jesus Christ His Son, who is His Word, proceeding from silence, who in all respects was well-pleasing to Him that sent Him.' The phrase 'proceeding from silence' is a difficult one. Some light may be thrown on it by ideas which we shall meet with in the next chapter. Here it will be sufficient to say that there is a contrast between God's self-revelation in the life of Jesus Christ, who for Ignatius as for the fourth Gospel, is the Logos, the Word, and the preceding ages when that revelation had not taken place. Barnabas finds a reference to Christ in the first chapter of Genesis: 'He is the Lord of all the world, to whom God said before the foundation of the world "let us make man in our image and likeness"'. It may be pointed out that we are not concerned with the correctness of Barnabas' interpretation. Few Old Testament scholars would be prepared to lay much stress on the plural in this verse—'let *us* make'. But Barnabas could apply this verse to Christ because of what he believed about Christ. The writer of the *Epistle to Diognetus* describes Christ as the Son or Child of God, as the very Artificer and Creator of the Universe, whom the almighty and invisible God sent to men: 'as a King sending a son, he sent him as God, he sent him as Man, he was saving and persuading when he sent him, not compelling, for compulsion is not an attribute of God'.

All this is, so far as it goes, clear enough. But we must not suppose that thought and expression were quite precise or that they were always in accord with later standards of true doctrine. There is a curious passage in the sermon which we call 2 Clement which may illustrate this. The preacher says, 'Now I imagine that you are not ignorant that the living Church is the body of Christ. For the Scripture says, "God made man male and female"; the male is Christ, the female is the Church'. Later writers would have thought this interpretation of a verse in the first chapter of Genesis one to be avoided. It is curious, by the way, that the preacher is here making use of the verse immediately succeeding the one which we have already noted as employed by Barnabas. But far the most remarkable instance of something like real confusion of thought comes in Hermas: puzzling though the language which he uses is, and obviously inappropriate for detailed discussion here, it deserves notice because of its relation to the doctrine of the Trinity. Now the Apostolic Fathers as a group continue the phraseology of the New Testament; that is, we do not find technical terms such as the word 'Trinity' itself, but we do find the association of God or the Father, and the Lord Jesus Christ and the Holy Spirit. Thus Clement, in his letter to Corinth, asks, 'Have we not one God, and one Christ, and one Spirit of Grace poured out upon us?' He assures them that 'as God lives and as the Lord Jesus Christ lives and the Holy Spirit, the faith and

hope of the elect,' those who obey God's commandments will gain salvation. Ignatius, using metaphorical
language which may strike us as more pretentious
than well-chosen, speaks of the Ephesian Christians as
'stones of the temple of the Father, made ready for
the building of God our Father, carried up to the
heights by the engine of Jesus Christ, that is the Cross,
and using as a rope the Holy Spirit'.

In the *Didaché* there is the command to baptize 'in
the name of the Father and of the Son and of the Holy
Spirit'. The account of the martyrdom of Polycarp
contains an ascription of glory to God, 'through the everlasting and heavenly high priest, Jesus Christ, Thy
beloved Child, through whom be glory to Thee with
Him and the Holy Spirit both now and for the ages
that are to come'.

Such then was the association of the three terms
Father, Son, and Holy Spirit. And, clearly, this
association demanded interpretation. What did it
mean that these three terms were brought together in
this way? Some time an answer would need to be
given; but that answer belonged to a later age than
the one we are now considering. And whereas, in this
first half of the second century, Jesus Christ appealed
not only to the hearts but also to the minds of Christians,
and we can say quite truly that there was a doctrine or
theology of His Person, it was not so, to anything like
the same extent, with regard to the Holy Spirit. The
question 'What think ye of Christ' was the question
which was at the centre of the difference between
Christians and everyone else, whether Jew or Gentile.
It was the question concerning the true place to be

given, in human thought and devotion, to the historic
Person Jesus, who was crucified under Pontius Pilate.
Everything turned on that. There was no similarly
arresting question as to the Holy Spirit. The gift of
the Holy Spirit was for those who already believed in
Jesus. What should be thought about the Holy Spirit
depended on what should be thought about Jesus.

Now Hermas was more of a popular religious writer
than of a theologian. His doctrine is given through
metaphors or pictures which can be very useful for
religious instruction, but are not necessarily the best
material for constructive theology. And Hermas certainly seems to identify the Holy Spirit with the Son
of God. He says quite definitely in one place that the
Holy Spirit, who in one of the visions had spoken to
him in the form of the Church, 'is the Son of God'.
And elsewhere, in the passage in which he speaks of
the Son of God as having cleansed the people's sins,
'labouring much and undergoing much toil'—a clear
reference to the earthly ministry of Jesus Christ—he
says that 'the Holy Spirit which goes forth, which
created all creation, did God make to dwell in the
flesh which He willed'. Indeed, in this chapter of the
Similitudes, Hermas pursues a line of thought which in
two ways is at variance both with later orthodoxy and
with the teaching of the Apostolic Fathers as a whole.
He identifies the Son and the Spirit, and makes what
today we might call a sharp distinction between Jesus
and Christ. He uses neither word, but he speaks of the
'flesh, in which the Holy Spirit dwelled', as serving
the Spirit well, and living nobly and labouring with
the Spirit, and as receiving for its reward the gift of

35   3-2

companionship with the Holy Spirit. And that seems to suggest a very curious Trinitarian doctrine in which Hermas once more shows himself as far from representative of normal Christian thought. But for all that he is not unimportant. He shows something of the difficulties which could present themselves to a Christian teacher. There is not the smallest reason for supposing that he wished to break away from the common faith of the Church. He realizes quite clearly and forcibly what great things Jesus had done; he wishes to emphasize the place of the Holy Spirit. But when he had to try to think things together, and to preserve true order and proportion in his thought, Hermas lacked what we should call the necessary philosophical equipment. The age of philosophical theology had not yet dawned. Not one of the Apostolic Fathers is a philosophical theologian, but Hermas stands alone in that his approach to a theology is so much off the true line when tested by the New Testament.

If we ask what conclusions as to the doctrine of Christ we may draw from these writings taken as a whole, we can, up to a certain point, give quite definite answers. Jesus Christ was believed to have pre-existed as the Son of God. Both the world's creation and the world's redemption from evil were ascribed to Him. There is nothing to suggest that He was regarded as a created being. When Ignatius says that Christ before the ages was with the Father, the natural inference is that Ignatius is affirming His eternity. Nor does the language used suggest that originally there was no personal distinction between the Father and the Son.

36

At the same time, the writers speak now and then in a way that implies some kind of subordination of Christ to the Father. Clement says that God 'chose out the Lord Jesus Christ and us through Him for a peculiar people'; Barnabas describes the Lord Jesus as 'having been prepared for this purpose, that when He appeared He might redeem our hearts from darkness'.

If the question be put—'Was the divinity of Christ part of the common faith of the Christian Church in the age to which the Apostolic Fathers belong?' the answer is 'Yes'. No distinction was made as to the blessings received from the Father and from Christ. Not only are the gifts which Christ brings to men God's gifts, which may be compatible with the idea of Christ as a kind of ambassador or plenipotentiary, but Christ's sufferings are the sufferings of God, His blood the blood of God—language which goes far beyond that idea. Again, there was no hesitation in substituting Christ for Jehovah in passages taken from the Old Testament, and there are instances of the reverse —sayings of Christ being referred to as sayings of God. To such thought and language only the notion that Jesus Christ pre-existed as the eternal divine Son of God does justice, the Son who is, as the fourth Gospel describes Him, the Logos or Word. But the truth to be preserved was manifold, and as yet there had been no adequate co-ordination and synthesis of ideas. For it was necessary to hold to the truth of the unity of God, the heritage derived from Hebrew Monotheism, to safeguard the personal distinction of the Son from the Father, and to remember that in the work both of creation and of redemption the Son did the Father's will.

CHAPTER III

In Defence of the Faith

I have already referred to the fact that before the end
of the first century the Roman Empire had adopted
an attitude of hostility to the Christian Church. As
a result of this, for considerably more than two hundred
years Christians were compelled to live in danger.
Active persecution was not continuous; and when it
arose, it was likely to be far worse in some districts than
in others. Much would depend on the character of the
particular Roman Governor on whom, in this or that
province, rested the responsibility of initiating criminal
proceedings and carrying out the desires of a persecuting Emperor. Moreover, by no means all the
Emperors wished to persecute the Church. Some were,
by nature, humane men; some were simply indifferent
to what they must have regarded as an unimportant
religious sect. The danger to the Church was probably
greatest when an Emperor of high conscientiousness,
determined to see the laws obeyed, was on the throne.
Such an one, especially if he had any feelings of intellectual contempt for Christianity, was likely to take
or to approve active measures against Christians. So it
was with the famous Emperor, Marcus Aurelius, the
philosopher king, a man of the highest morality,
utterly devoted to the welfare of the State. It was in
his reign, in the latter part of the second century, that
the Christian Church in south France suffered one of
the fiercest of persecutions. An account of it was sent

38

from the south of France to Christians in Asia Minor. It is a long and most dramatic narrative. It introduces us to one of the most famous of early Christian martyrs—the slave-girl Blandina. And it is from this document that we learn that when the local authorities sent to Rome to get the Emperor's decision on what ought to be done with the imprisoned Christians, the reply that came from Marcus Aurelius was 'execution for all except such as should renounce their faith'. So the Governor ordered that Roman citizens should be beheaded, and the rest thrown to the wild beasts. Something like a tradition grew up among Christians that only the notoriously bad Emperors persecuted the Church: but that was not the case. Nero, the first persecuting Emperor, could answer to that title, and there were others who were no honour to the exalted position which they occupied. But that was not true of Marcus Aurelius in the second century, or of Decius in the third, or of Diocletian in the fourth.

But why did persecution take place? It is not sufficient to reply 'because Christianity was an unauthorized religion': that does not explain the ferocity which at times marked the persecutions. Moreover, there is the further question, 'Why was Christianity refused a place among the religions and cults which existed within the wide tolerance of the Empire?' For the Empire was far from inclined to persecute where religion was concerned. There was something like an official State religion in which the existence of the old Graeco-Roman deities was recognized; and there was the worship of the reigning Emperor as of a god living and ruling on the earth. Some Emperors took this cult more seriously than others, and it was more popular in the Asiatic than in the European part of the Empire. Otherwise, the State exercised a policy of benevolent neutrality. One may think of it as keeping the ring for the professors of different creeds. But within that ring the Christians had no place. Why? The answer is that Christianity was misunderstood on the intellectual and religious sides, and maligned on the moral side. The latter fact is the more important; but the extraordinary charges brought against Christians in regard to their moral conduct were bound up with a misunderstanding of the nature of the Christian religion. To that I shall soon come. The attacks upon Christian morality included treasonable designs against the State, horrible orgies in worship, and general malevolence. In two documents proceeding from non-Christian sources this attitude comes to light. First, in his *Annals*, the famous Roman historian Tacitus refers to Christians in connexion with the great fire of Rome which occurred when Nero was Emperor. The passage is so noteworthy that a translation of its greater part will not be out of place. The only thing that needs to be said by way of introduction to it is that there was a widespread belief in Rome that the Emperor himself had been responsible for the conflagration, that he might gaze upon the spectacle of the burning city. Tacitus continues:

So, to stifle the report, Nero substituted in his own place and condemned to punishments of the most refined cruelty men whom the populace hated for their monstrous crimes. They were called Christians. Christ, from whom they took their name, was put to death by order of the procurator Pontius Pilate in the reign of Tiberius. For the time the detestable superstition was checked, but it broke out again, not only in Judaea, the original home of this evil, but also in the city of Rome. It is customary for every kind of atrocious and shameful vice to find its way to the Capital and to gain adherents. First of all some were arrested and confessed to the crime, then on their information a vast number were convicted not so much of the crime of arson as of hatred of the human race.

Tacitus goes on to describe the character of their deaths: some were crucified and set on fire to illuminate the Emperor's gardens, while Nero himself was present and took part in a circus exhibition. 'Hence', Tacitus concludes, 'pity was felt for these men, wretches though they were and deserving of the severest punishments, for it was felt that they were being put to death not in the public interests, but to satisfy the cruelty of an individual.' It is an extraordinary passage. Tacitus was a Roman aristocrat. He hated the Empire which had taken the place of the old Roman republic. He hated and despised Nero. He hated also what seemed to him superstition, especially when it was foreign superstition. He knew something about the origin of Christianity; but of the character of Christianity he was wholly ignorant. To us, with the New Testament in our hands, his account of Christian morals seems merely ludicrous. But no book of the New Testament is likely ever to have been in the hands of Tacitus, and he may never have had half an hour's conversation with a Christian. His attitude seems to be—'The Christians were not guilty of the great fire, but as all kinds of crimes lay to their charge there was no reason to pity their fate—except for the fact that they were the scapegoats of a tyrant anxious to save his skin and to gratify his lust for cruelty'!

The other document is a letter written by Pliny, Governor of Bithynia in the north of Asia Minor, to the great and noble Emperor Trajan. Its date is A.D. III. Pliny wanted to know what to do about the Christians in his province. Were they to be punished for being Christians or for the crimes associated with Christianity? His difficulty was that though he could not induce those who came before his court and were really Christians to abjure Christianity, he could not discover any actual crime of which they were guilty. Some who had once been, but were no longer, Christians, did worship the Emperor's statue in court and cursed Christ. But still Pliny could find no evidence of penal offences. These men, so he tells the Emperor,

affirmed that this had been the sum total of their fault or error: they had been accustomed on a stated day to come together before daybreak, to sing by turns a hymn to Christ as a God, and to bind themselves by an oath, not for the commission of any crime, but for the avoidance of theft, robbery, and adultery; the oath bound them also not to break their word and not to repudiate a deposit when it was demanded of them.

Pliny had made use of torture (a practice allowed under Roman law), but from the two deaconesses subjected to it he discovered nothing but a 'wicked and extravagant superstition'. It is clear that Pliny did regard the profession of Christianity as a punishable offence; Christians who were brought before him and refused to deny their faith he sent to be executed; they were guilty, in his own words, of 'stubbornness and unbending obstinacy'. It is equally clear that, apart from their faith, he knew of nothing against them. He might have said of them what Festus and Agrippa said of St Paul, 'This man doeth nothing worthy of death or of bonds'. Trajan's reply points the same way: he tells Pliny that if Christians are accused and convicted— one must supply the words 'of being Christians'—they are to be punished: but they are not to be sought out— a quite unintelligible command if the Emperor had believed that Christians were guilty of the crimes popularly attributed to them. No wonder that the Christian writer Tertullian was to indulge in some grim sarcasm at the expense of the inconsistency of this policy!

But why were Christians unpopular? A number of causes contributed to this fact. To begin with, they stood aloof from a great deal of the social life of the day. That was inevitable. For social life was permeated in various ways with the recognition of idols, and for a Christian any kind of accommodation to idolatry was a sin of the gravest order. Add to this fact of unsociableness, as it must have been regarded, the fact that Christians did not throw open their worship to all and sundry. The most sacred mysteries of that worship and of the faith which inspired it were for believers. Moreover, as freedom to worship God according to their consciences was not granted to Christians, worship had to take place in secret. One need only mention the catacombs of Rome. Such an atmosphere is too favourable to the growth of sinister stories; even in our own day the Jews in Eastern Europe have suffered from similar suspicions. Moreover, Christians were religiously exclusive. It was an age when adherence to one cult did not normally imply condemnation of others. But Christians claimed that theirs was the one true religion and they would have nothing to do with any other. Particularly unpopular in some places must have been their refusal to join in worship of the reigning Emperor, to acknowledge him to be 'Our Lord and God', to burn incense before his statue. This could easily be regarded as a proof of bad citizenship. The greatness of the Empire was centred in the Emperor, and those who would not pay the tribute of worship to his divinity were, surely, plotters against the security of the State. Christians had repudiated the old gods, and though they professed to adore a spiritual and invisible Creator, at the centre of their cult was one who had been condemned and put to death as a criminal by a Roman Governor. The Cross was a stumbling-block to the Jews, and to the Greeks foolishness. Those words of St Paul remained true, and still the Church, like the great Apostle of the Gentiles, preached Christ crucified 'to us who are called, both Jews and Greeks, the power of God and the wisdom of God'.

It is against this background that we need to review the work and teaching of that group of Christian writers of the second century who are called the Apologists. Defences of Christianity went on into the third century and even beyond, but the earlier writers can be treated as a unity by themselves. Some of the defences have not survived, or we possess only fragments. But enough has come down to us in the way of completed works to understand the general purpose of these authors and to estimate the nature of the contribution they made to Christian thought. They were in a number of instances men of considerable intellectual attainments. The author of the earliest 'apology' (to use the technical term) which we possess was Aristides, an Athenian philosopher, who addressed it to the Emperor Antoninus Pius. This Emperor, who reigned from A.D. 138 to A.D. 161, was also the recipient of two 'apologies' from the most famous representative of this group, Justin, often called, in view of his fate, Justin Martyr. Justin had been a philosopher, though attached to no particular school, and, as a sign of his belief that in becoming a Christian he had not ceased to be a philosopher, he still wore the philosopher's cloak. Yet another philosopher, Athenagoras of Athens, inscribed his defence to Marcus Aurelius and his son Commodus, when they were reigning as joint-Emperors between A.D. 177 and A.D. 180. About the same time, or a little earlier, Theophilus, Bishop of Antioch, wrote three books to a certain Autolycus, while, earlier still, a disciple of Justin's, a certain Tatian, an Assyrian, produced his Oration to the Greeks. Two great Christian writers, who contributed defences of Christianity, were the North African Tertullian, and the Alexandrian Origen. But they were later in date, and though we shall meet with them again they are not to be included in the particular group we are considering.

The Apologists, in their writings, had two objects in view. They wanted, first of all, to refute the calumnies to which the Christian Church was exposed, to show that the Christians were neither a seditious nor a vicious people, and to convince those whom they addressed that the policy of persecution rested on no rational and defensible basis. Secondly, they desired to make plain what Christians really did believe about God and the world, and to commend Christianity as the supremely true religion to the educated intelligence of the day. Their purpose was, therefore, essentially a conciliatory one. They wished to show that Christianity was neither politically dangerous, nor morally debased, nor intellectually contemptible. Some of them could use very violent language in denouncing the absurdities and obscenities of heathen polytheism. But the substance of their appeal is not affected by that fact. And we must remember that, in respect of their theology, they were particularly concerned to emphasize those elements in the Christian faith which would especially appeal to educated or philosophical pagans. If one were asked to express in a phrase the light in which the Apologists regarded Christianity, and which they aimed at imparting to those whom they addressed, the answer would be—'As the true philosophy'. Christianity was worthy of no less attention than Platonism or Stoicism or any other philosophy. Like them it was concerned with questions of universal importance. But, unlike them, it was free from inconsistencies and absurdities, and adopted an attitude of uncompromising opposition to all idolatry.

Let us see how the Apologists understood the reason

for this superiority in Christianity. We may say quite briefly that they based the truth and preeminence of the Christian philosophy on the fact of divine revelation. The great pagan philosophies were man-made; in them was to be seen the speculations of the human mind. The Apologists differed a good deal among themselves in the views they took of man's power, by his own native intelligence, to make some approach to truth. Some of them held that man was necessarily drawn towards Christianity by his possession of reason. Here the importance of the expression Logos is very great. At the beginning of St John's Gospel the Greek word Logos is translated as 'Word' in our English versions. This may be the best translation, since St John's notion of Jesus Christ as the Word of God who had become incarnate and lived among men may have its roots in the Old Testament idea of the Word of God. In that case the Greek word Logos was used by him as the equivalent of the Hebrew expression Memra, which quite definitely means 'word'. But Logos could also mean 'reason', and was used in that sense in Greek philosophy. Men were rational beings because they possessed Logos (Reason). Therefore it was not difficult for some of the Apologists to see in the reason of man an inspiration or spark of that divine Logos who had become incarnate as the historical Jesus Christ. There are two short passages of Justin in his first *Apology* which are worth quoting in this connexion. They show a very remarkable liberality of outlook and make it plain that a Christian teacher could do justice to the true and noble elements in pagan philosophy. In the first passage Justin ascribes the death of the famous Athenian philosopher Socrates to the influence of evil demons whom Justin identifies with the gods of heathenism. They were the cause of the fate which befell Socrates, just as they were the cause of the persecution of Christians. Because he tried to lead men away from demons,

the demons themselves, through the agency of men who delighted in evil, caused him to be put to death as a godless and impious person, saying that he was introducing strange divinities: similarly they contrive that the same thing should happen in our case. For not only among the Greeks, through Socrates, were these things [he is thinking of various kinds of wickedness] condemned by reason, but also among the barbarians by the Reason Himself taking shape and being made man and being called Jesus Christ.

I may explain that the expression 'barbarian' was the regular way in which a Greek described those who were not Greeks: its best equivalent is 'foreigner'.

The other passage is a very famous one. Justin is meeting a possible objection. People might say 'as Christ was born only one hundred and fifty years ago, and His teaching was till then unknown, those who lived before that time cannot be held responsible for the character of their lives: the truth had not been revealed to them'. Justin will not allow the validity of this objection. His reply is

We were taught that Christ is the firstborn of God, and we have previously shown that He is the Reason in which every race of men shared. So those who lived with reason are Christians, even though they were accounted Godless, and I may give as instances

48

among the Greeks Socrates and Heraclitus and persons
like to them.

Justin, then, believed that all men possessed a seed
of the divine Reason. But what they possessed they
did not safeguard. Hence came in all the errors of
pagan thought and pagan religion; hence came the
need for the appearance of 'our teacher Christ'. And
in His case there was something far more than the
presence of a seed of the Reason, for He was the whole
Reason incarnate.

All the Apologists were convinced of this necessity
for divine revelation, if mankind was not to stray far
from the truth. Not all of them agreed with Justin as
to there being a seed of the divine Reason in the mind
of man. Some took a much less favourable view of
human nature than was the case with Justin. But it is
the agreement on the extreme importance of revelation
which needs emphasis. It is a curious thing that with
all their stress upon revelation the religious truths to
which the Apologists paid special attention are not
peculiar to Christianity. They have been and are held
in other religions. They are the doctrines of the existence of one almighty God who is the Creator of the
world, of the need for a good life, and of judgment to
come. But we can easily understand why the Apologists made so much of these doctrines. They were living
in the midst of a pagan society which accepted the
existence of many gods, which was often unaware of
any connexion between religion and morality, and had
no vital belief that men would be called to account for
their evil deeds. And what the Apologists wished to
make plain to their pagan neighbours was their assur-

ance of certain fundamental truths about God and human life. And their assurance rested on the revelation of these truths in the teaching of Christ. They realized that these truths had been known before Christ came. Athenagoras could say that the Christian doctrine of God had been propounded by the most distinguished philosophers. Tatian remarks that Christian doctrine gives us 'not what we had not received, but what, though we had received it, we were through error unable to retain'. Even Theophilus, who goes so far as to say that the old poets and philosophers were inspired by demons, admits that they taught what was true when the demons departed from them. Then they returned to sobriety and displayed a knowledge of the sovereignty of God and of His judgment of the world. Thus we may say that the form which the teaching of the Apologists took was dictated by the state of the world in which they lived and by the kind of appeal which they wished to make.

I must now say something of the way in which these writers thought of the divine Logos or Reason. They all taught that the Logos had become incarnate as Jesus Christ. So we may think of them as continuing and emphasizing the teaching given in the Prologue to the fourth Gospel. This use of the idea of the Logos is characteristic of them and distinguishes them, as a group, from the Apostolic Fathers. Ignatius, indeed, spoke of Christ as the Logos of God, but both he and the other Apostolic Fathers are much more inclined to describe Christ as the Son or Child of God. We may say that, after the fourth Gospel, the Apologists are the first Christian writers to give to the doctrine of the Logos a foremost place in Christian theology. How then did they conceive of the Logos and of His relation to God before the Incarnation?

They taught that God always has Logos, Reason, within Himself. The Logos therefore, is eternal and uncreated, essentially one with God. Theophilus speaks of the Logos as being always immanent in the heart of God. But they do not seem to have thought of this immanent Logos as possessing what we should call a distinct personality. There are statements of which the natural meaning is that the Logos became personally distinct from God when God determined to create the world. Then the Logos was no longer the immanent Reason of God. He became the uttered Word. He 'leapt forth', to use a strong metaphor of Tatian. Justin, in his dialogue with the Jew, Trypho, speaks of the Logos, whom he there describes as 'this power', as having been begotten by the Father. At the same time, Justin is careful to repudiate any materialistic interpretation of this phrase, as though it meant that when the Logos was begotten the essence or being of the Father was in any way divided or impaired. But Justin was conscious of theological difficulties. His language can approach to a description of the Logos as a second or another God, next after the supreme Father. But he knew that the doctrine of the One God must not be surrendered, and he tries to preserve it by adding that the word 'another' does not imply any division of will between the Father and the Logos; the distinction is simply a numerical distinction. No one, whatever his own point of view, will think that Justin is very satisfactory in his language, or adequate in his explanation. But in order to do justice to him or to the other Apologists we must remember that they felt bound to assert both the unity of the Godhead and the divinity of the Logos. Moreover, while they believed that the Logos was eternal they did not think that His Sonship was eternal. Rather did they think of the Logos as becoming the Son of God and, as such, personally distinct from the Father, at what we should call a moment in eternity. A professional philosopher would not pass such a phrase, but it is fairly descriptive of the thought of the Apologists. Yet one of them, the philosopher Athenagoras, tried to reach a more satisfactory position. He lays more stress on the Sonship of the Logos and speaks of the Trinity, though he does not use the word, in a manner which is remarkable at that stage in the development of theology. He meets the charge that Christians are atheists. That was a false charge. Christians, he affirms, proclaim 'God who is Father, and the Son who is God and the Holy Spirit, and show the power which lies in the unity and the distinction which lies in the order'. Again he speaks of 'the Son being in the Father and the Father in the Son by the unity and power of the Spirit'. The actual word 'Trinity', in the Greek 'Trias', occurs first in Theophilus, who says that three days of the creation were 'types of the Trinity, of God, and of His Word and of His Wisdom'.

It is, I think, clear that, from the standpoint of later Christian theology, the Apologists were in difficulties because they were inclined to subordinate the idea of the Son of God to the idea of the Logos of God. That is,

He could be regarded as first of all the Logos, and then afterwards as becoming the Son. And the idea of Logos, of Reason, either in God or in man, does not naturally carry with it the idea of distinct personality. I do not naturally think of my reason as personally distinct from myself. It was a great thing to try to meet philosophical heathen on their own ground, to point out that the philosophical notion of the Logos of which so much had been made in the Stoic system was familiar to Christians. But there was a danger of depending too much upon and trying to make too much of one philosophical notion. One may feel at times that the Apologists would have done better to rely more directly on the New Testament. It would be unfair to them to suggest that they came near to transforming Christianity into a philosophy; what they wished to do was to give philosophical expression to Christian truth. But it would be proper to say that the distinctive religious strength and appeal of Christianity is not foremost in their works. This may be illustrated in two ways. The Apologists as a whole lay little stress on the historical personality of Jesus. There is an absence of the kind of devotion which is so markedly present in Ignatius. It is not that they were indifferent to the Gospel history. But the stress falls on the fulfilment of Old Testament prophecy in the facts of His life, rather than on His life as the revelation of the goodness and graciousness of God. But again we must make allowance for the circumstances—the Apologists were stating or arguing the truth of the Christian case against pagan unbelievers, or, in Justin's dialogue with Trypho, against a Jew. Yet even so it must strike us as very curious that neither Tatian nor Theophilus ever uses the personal names 'Jesus' and 'Christ'.

Then, further, the Apologists make much more of Christianity as a religion of revelation than as a religion of redemption. One may put it in this way: in the first chapter of St John's Gospel, Christ, the Logos incarnate, is spoken of as the source of grace and truth, or, again, as dwelling among men 'full of grace and truth'. In the Apologists the emphasis falls much more on the truth than on the grace. Christ is the supreme Teacher rather than the world's Redeemer. And however rightly this aspect of Christ as the one who has given the true teaching about God and man is made prominent, one cannot but feel that from the New Testament standpoint there is a grave lack of proportion when little is made of the other aspect, when the blessings of the forgiveness of sins, of new strength, and of communion with God are comparatively neglected. The Cross of Christ, which has so central a place in the New Testament, and has meant so much in Christian experience, has no corresponding importance in the writings of the Apologists. Justin is here more adequate than the others. In his second *Apology* he speaks of Christians as worshipping and loving, next to God, the Logos, 'since for us He became Man that He might share our sufferings and effect our cure'. But, taking the group as a whole, one would describe them as implying that men are redeemed by being given and by following the true doctrine whereby they can gain freedom from the errors introduced by evil, demonic powers.

Nevertheless, the Apologists well served their generation in the history of the Christian Church. They realized that Christians must be prepared to give a reason for the faith that was in them, that Christianity had a message to man's intellect. They opened out a path along which greater men than themselves were to tread and reach results beyond their own power to achieve. Even their failures were not fruitless. The failures and errors of one age can be of real service to the cause of truth in another.

CHAPTER IV

Necessary Controversy and Constructive Theology

We have now seen something of the defences of Christianity put forward in the second century by the group of writers who are called the Apologists. They faced the danger which threatened the Christian Church as a result of the hostility of the State and of the widespread misunderstandings of the character of the Christian religion. But that was not the only danger at that time. There was another, which was both more subtle and more serious. That was the danger to the true nature and purity of the Christian faith resulting from the ideas and the influence of the persons known as Gnostics. The Gnostics were people who claimed, as their name implies, to possess knowledge. They put forward their knowledge as something superior to the common faith of the Church. Or, one may say, that they taught that the real meaning of the faith was to be grasped only when it was interpreted in accordance with their own superior knowledge.

We know the names of a number of the Gnostic teachers, and a considerable amount about their doctrines. In justice to them we must remember that we know them mainly through the writings of their opponents, and that controversialists, however fairminded, are seldom able to present quite adequately all the features, still less the inner spirit, of a system to which they are opposed. Still, there is not much doubt as to the main lines of Gnostic teaching, and it is these which I shall try to make clear. I would say by way of preliminary that Gnostic teachers and Gnostic schools or fellowships sprang up in various parts of the Empire. They were most common in the East. Some of the most important flourished in Syria and in Egypt, but they penetrated into the West, as far as France. There was a good deal of Gnosticism at one time in the Rhone Valley. As to their relation to the Church one cannot always be certain. But some Gnostic leaders were, for a while, members of the Church in their respective localities, and later either withdrew from the Church or were expelled. But whatever their precise relation, their desire was to leaven the Church with their own doctrines. And in the attempt to do this they wrote 'Gospels' which they ascribed to one or other of the Apostles of Christ, and referred to as giving authority for their own teachings. One of the most interesting discoveries of the late nineteenth century was that of fragments of the so-called Gospel according to Peter. These fragments deal with the trial, passion, and resurrection of Christ, and there are passages which make it clear that this Gospel was composed under the influence of the Gnostic view which denied that Christ really suffered, when crucified, and even went on to deny the reality of His human nature. To this point I shall return later. Besides these fictitious Gospels, the Gnostics laid claim to the possession of secret traditions which authorized their teachings. One of the Gnostic works which we possess is called *Pistis Sophia*, that is, *Believing Wisdom*, and the teaching given is based on instructions given by the Lord after His resurrection.

Now the peril to Christianity from the side of Gnosticism was that the substance of the Christian faith should be transformed through the influence of ideas which in some cases were directly opposed to the Christian good news about God and man. The Gnostics owed a great deal to ideas of a semi-religious, semi-philosophical character, which were widely diffused, especially in the East. Had Gnosticism prevailed the character of Christianity would have been radically changed. It would not be true to say that Christianity would have ceased to be a religion and would have become a speculative philosophy. For the Gnostic leaders were genuinely interested in religion, and though they were capable of a great deal of very curious speculation they would hardly rank as philosophers, if by philosophy we mean the kind of thinking which produced the great Greek philosophical systems. But the religion which a victorious Gnosticism would have produced would have been very different from the religion of the New Testament.

To get at the roots of Gnosticism we must understand its attitude towards the oldest and most mysterious problem in the world, the problem of evil. Now, the pre-Christian world outside Judaism had been inclined to insist on the difference between spirit and matter, and to ascribe to matter not only an inferior rank as compared with spirit but even something of an inherently evil character or tendency. In Greek thought this contrast between spirit and matter did not go to extremes. Yet Plato, in his great work the *Timaeus*, does regard matter as a hindrance to God in the work of creation. He did not think of matter as owing its existence to God; it was eternal, in itself formless and without definite quality. But an element of irrationality adhered to it, and for a Greek anything irrational had the nature of evil. Accordingly a world formed out of matter would necessarily lack perfection. The fact, moreover, that matter is something which lacks constancy, that the forms into which it is moulded come and pass away, would prejudice it in the eyes of a Greek thinker accustomed to the contrast between the One and the Many. Unity and Goodness were for a Greek naturally associated with one another, while the manifoldness was akin to evil. A different standpoint was taken up in the Persian religion of Zoroastrianism. There we have the forces of good and evil in active warfare for supremacy in the world, and identified with two rival deities. Still further East, in Indian thought, matter was regarded as the lowest form of existence, indeed, not real existence at all, but *Maya*, illusion, and therefore evil.

In the world of the second century A.D. what is known as religious syncretism, the tendency to the amalgamation of various religious and philosophical notions, was very common. The Gnostic movement is one of the instances of it. It is needless to ask, even if we felt sure that a satisfactory answer would be forthcoming, precisely whence were derived the ideas which we meet with in Gnosticism, or how they welded these ideas into a unity. But the point to emphasize is that the Gnostic systems circled round the fact of evil and the need for redemption from evil; evil was to be found in close association with matter, and redemption involved the freeing of the spirit from the entanglements of matter. For the Gnostics there could be no redemption or purifying of matter itself, and while much stress was laid on the redeeming work of Christ, He was not viewed, as St Paul had viewed Him, as the Redeemer of the whole man, spirit *and* body.

Now this conception of matter as evil inevitably involved the Gnostics in difficulties as to the relation between God and the world. In Hebrew thought as we find it in the Old Testament, there was a perfectly clear distinction between God and the world. The emphasis falls on God's transcendence. He is other than the world, infinitely distinct. There is little approach to the thought of God's immanence in the world, which many philosophers of religion would regard as in no way opposed to the idea of divine transcendence, but as necessary if the whole truth is to be stated. In so far as the Old Testament finds a place for the conception of the divine immanence it is in its teaching concerning the Spirit of God. But the stress upon God's transcendence of the world did not prevent the Hebrew writers from ascribing to God the creation of the world. Indeed, this was a fixed point in their thought, and the more conscious they became of the unity of God, the more confidently did they attribute to that one God the creation of the world. For it did not occur to them to think of matter as evil. There was no difficulty in regarding God as the Creator of the world. It was only when Hebrew thought became to some extent affected by Greek ideas that the belief in direct creation by God caused any difficulty. The Gnostics were in a quite different position. They could not believe that God, who was pure Spirit, could be the Creator of the material world. What then about the Old Testament, and the view taken there that the world was the work of Jehovah? The Gnostics did not deny this; they allowed that Jehovah was the Creator; but they went on to a doctrine as to Jehovah which involved a very sharp separation between themselves and the Old Testament. Jehovah, they said, was the Creator, but He was not the supreme God: a divine being of a kind He might be, but not more than that. At best He was an agent of the supreme God in creation. So in Plato we find the notion of intermediary divine beings in the work of creation, and we may think of the rôle ascribed to angels in later Judaism. But the Creator could also be regarded as an enemy of the supreme God, a hostile power. Some Gnostic teachers went to the length of reversing the moral estimates attached to various persons in the Old Testament: those who appear there as faithful servants of Jehovah such teachers condemned, and reserved their approbation for those who, because of their disloyalty to Jehovah, are, in the Old Testament, ranked as evildoers. One of the most famous of the Gnostic teachers, Marcion, the son of a Christian bishop in north Asia Minor, held that Jehovah was just but not good; that He was God but not the supreme God, and was ignorant of the existence of the supreme God till Christ, that true God's Son, came to teach men about His Father.

The Gnostic doctrines concerning the creation of the world are the most speculative and fanciful parts of their systems. It is sufficient to say that creation was never regarded as in any way the work of the supreme

God, and that some kind of inherent flaw or error was often supposed to be a mark of the created world. Such a world needed to be put right; or rather, it would be truer to say, the spirits of men in the world needed to be freed from the evil of their environment. To this end Christ, the Redeemer, came into the world. He came from the supreme God. Marcion taught that He was the Son of God: other Gnostics taught that He was a pre-existent being, one of those spiritual existences described as 'aeons'. He came to give the true knowledge of God and to liberate men from their slavery to the Creator. But here, once more, the Gnostic belief in the fundamental contrast between spirit and matter worked adversely to the New Testament doctrine that Jesus Christ was come in the flesh, that He took the reality of human nature. Two strains in Gnostic teaching may here be distinguished. Some said outright that the humanity of Christ had no existence: it was appearance, not reality. This is the position known as 'docetism', from the Greek word meaning 'to appear'. Ignatius of Antioch came across teaching of this type and spoke his mind about it, especially about the denial of the reality of the sufferings of Christ. Jesus Christ, he tells the believers at Smyrna, 'suffered all these things for us that we might be saved: and He truly suffered, even as also He truly raised Himself; it is not as some unbelievers say, that His passion was mere appearance—it is they who exist merely in appearance'. The other form of Gnosticism allowed the reality of the human nature of Christ, but sharply distinguished between Jesus and Christ. Jesus was the name given to the human being upon whom the Christ descended at His baptism, and whom the Christ left before the crucifixion. We can see an instance of this in the Gospel according to Peter. There, on the Cross, in the words of the author, 'the Lord cried out, saying, My power, My power, why hast thou forsaken me?' But the author also held the view that there was no real suffering, for earlier on he says that the Jews crucified the Lord between two malefactors, 'but He held His peace, as having no pain'. Further, at least one great school of Gnostics was unable to affirm that Christ's redeeming work could avail for all men. In some men the material element was too strong: they were incapable of salvation: in others spirit was so predominant that their salvation was certain: midway came those who were called the 'psychic ones', who might either rise to the level of the spiritual, or sink into the ranks of the material. And not only the possibilities of salvation but practical ethics were affected by the low valuation set on matter. The material element in man represented something worthless and evil. Salvation was for the spirit alone. How then should the body be treated? The greatest Gnostic leaders taught the necessity for a stern control of the body. The more its impulses were suppressed, the greater the advance in the life of the spirit. Thus, human conduct should be rigorously ascetic. But there was another possibility, and it would seem that it was sometimes adopted. We need to be specially watchful against easy credence of charges of immorality. Yet some of the Gnostics gained an evil name. In so far as any of them were guilty of immoral practices, their defence would have been that the body and the use made of it were of no importance, and that whatever happened in the sphere of the body could not affect the well-being of the spirit.

These positions taken together, as they develop from a common root, amount to a world-view far removed from anything we can find in the books of the New Testament, or in the common teaching of the early Church. And if the Gnostics had gained control of the Church one result would have immediately followed. The relation of the Church and of Christianity to the Old Testament would have been cut clean away. And that would have meant the undermining of the historical position of Christianity. For it is the simple truth to say that neither Jesus Christ nor the Christian religion in its origin and early development can be understood apart from the Old Testament. Marcion is very illuminating here. He ruled out all connexion between the Old Testament and the Christian Gospel. With Christ and the Father of Christ, the supreme God, the Old Testament had nothing to do at all. Marcion taught that Christ suddenly appeared from God, in the fifteenth year of the Emperor Tiberias, without a human birth, to tell the truth about God to the Jews who mistakenly supposed that the world's creator, their God Jehovah, was the one true God. The Jews, the servants of Jehovah, put Christ to death. But they could not prevent His rising again. Yet error still continued: the original apostles taught that Christ was the Messiah to whom some passages of the Old Testament looked forward; they did not realise that the Old Testament and its prophecies had nothing whatever to do with Christ the crucified Saviour. So St Paul was called to be the true Apostle, to correct the mistakes of the first Apostles, and to break the link between the Gospel and the religion of the Jews. Of which scheme of thought one is bound to say that its ingenuity is more remarkable than its historical sense or its faithfulness to facts. It is no wonder that Marcion had to have his particular body of sacred writings. He accepted the Gospel of St Luke, with the first two chapters omitted: in them the Messianic hopes of the Jews were much too prominent for his purposes. He further accepted ten epistles of St Paul, though in them too he found things which he had to cut out. As Tertullian remarked, Marcion's method of criticism was the penknife. His disciples reverenced a work of Marcion called *Antitheses*, 'Contrasts', that is, between Judaism and Christianity. Yet with all Marcion's perverseness he was profoundly right in one respect. He saw that Christianity was essentially a religion of redemption, and that the greatest aspect of the work of Christ was His character as Redeemer. And in that he was a true disciple of St Paul.

The Gnostics failed. Christian theology might be in a comparatively undeveloped state, but at least it was following the path of true and natural development, whereas Gnosticism was reactionary revolution. It meant the abandonment of the characteristic New Testament positions and the substitution of ideas derived from pre-Christian orientalism. But the Gnostic controversy had its positive and constructive value. It compelled Christian thinkers to go deeper into the significance of the Christian faith, and to draw out more fully the meaning of Christian doctrines. When we come to men like Irenaeus, Bishop of Lyons in France, and Tertullian the Carthaginian presbyter, who brought to the statement and defence of Christian doctrine the dialectical acuteness which he had developed as a lawyer, we have reached a stage in Christian theology beyond that of the Apostolic Fathers and the Apologists. Of these two men something must now be said.

Irenaeus is one of the most representative of Christian thinkers. He was born in Asia Minor where, in his youth, he had been a hearer of Polycarp. Later he went to South France and became Bishop of Lyons after the great persecution which took place in the time of Marcus Aurelius; he was well acquainted with the Church in Rome. Without being a thinker of the first order, he was a very able and well-balanced theologian. He lacked the brilliance and the fire of Tertullian, but was a no less powerful opponent of the Gnostics. He was one of the men who may lack the higher philosophical qualities, but who see the real point at issue and keep it well to the front. Such men do not belong to the class of pioneers in thought but they have their own special place as consolidators of positions already reached. Irenaeus' great work is entitled *Against Heresies*, and is in five books. It is a reply to the Gnostics, and we can see how his own theological emphasis comes by way of reaction against typical Gnostic positions. Against the Gnostic disparagement of the Creator and introduction of a different higher God, Irenaeus insists that the Creator of the world is the supreme God and the Father of Christ. Like the Apologists he makes much of the idea of revelation, but he goes deeper than the Apologists in teaching that all the qualities of God may be summed up in love, and that love is the motive of God's revelation of Himself. Apart from revelation, God cannot be known: 'No one', he says, 'can know God, unless God has taught him'. And that revelation comes to its climax in Jesus Christ the Son of God who has been made Son of Man. Irenaeus lays the stress upon the historical Person Jesus Christ in a way foreign to some of the Apologists. It is not that he has turned away from the Logos doctrine. Irenaeus is as sure as were his predecessors that Christ is the divine Logos or Reason incarnate. But probably from his own preference, and certainly from the exigencies of the Gnostic controversy, he had to speak far more directly about the historical Jesus. He had to make it clear that the Gnostic view of the Incarnation, whatever form it took, was incompatible with the foundation truths of Christianity. There could be no separation of Jesus from Christ. The Church believed in one Lord Jesus Christ. He speaks as strongly as Ignatius of the reality of Christ's human experiences. Christ could reveal the Father because He was the divine Son, in whom the Father could be seen. Irenaeus seems to think of this as true not only in connexion with the historical life of Christ, but eternally. Always is the Father revealed in the Son. Irenaeus' doctrine of the Trinity is much fuller than that of any other second-century writer. How the Trinity is to be understood in relation to the unity of God is the kind of speculative question on which he does not enter: yet he certainly thinks of the Son and of the Holy Spirit as eternal along with the Father. The very metaphor he

uses points that way. Of both the Son or Logos and of
the Spirit Irenaeus uses the description 'the hand of
the Father'. It has been said of his doctrine that it
implies a subordination of the Son and the Spirit to the
Father. And such a word may be allowed if it is meant
to imply that Irenaeus assigns a certain priority to the
Father within the Godhead; also he teaches that man's
approach to God is through the Spirit and the Son to
the Father. But any interpretation of Irenaeus which
would suggest that he thought of the Son and the
Spirit as creatures would be completely mistaken. It
is in his doctrine of the redemption of man through
the coming of Christ that Irenaeus shows his most
characteristic thought. Just as he traced God's will to
reveal Himself to the motive of God's love, so he traced
the fact of the Incarnation to the love which the Son of
God had for the men whom He had created. And
Irenaeus saw in the Incarnation itself, in the fact that
the Son of God had become Man, the reality of redemption. Christ in His own Person united man to God; in
the preface to the fifth book he says that 'Christ became what we are in order to make us that which He
is Himself'. This is to be understood as a doctrine of
the elevation of human nature to a higher level by the
union in Christ of the human with the divine. It is
not a pantheistic doctrine of a fusion of divinity with
humanity. Irenaeus could not have entertained such
an idea. Nor is it a doctrine that every man can become a Christ. That again is a way of thinking quite
foreign to Irenaeus or to early Christian theology.
What we have to realize is that human nature could be
spoken of at that time in a way which many people

today would find difficult. Yet in some ways Irenaeus strikes a very modern note, as when he speaks of man as being created with the possibility of perfection, but as unable to attain to perfection at first, like a child who cannot assimilate strong food, or as when he describes Christ as summing up in His own Person that which man was intended to be.

It is natural to think of Irenaeus as a great Churchman; Tertullian is far more difficult to classify. He is one of the most remarkable personalities in early Church history, one of those who put themselves into their writings in such a way that one feels that one cannot be mistaken as to the kind of man he was. Irenaeus, when he writes against the Gnostics, is detached and impersonal. We realize the strength of his convictions but we do not know much more about himself. Tertullian is one of the most personal of writers: in all sorts of ways he throws light upon himself. The man is always coming through the opinions, and anyone who wants to know the kind of person this really extraordinary man was could not do better than read the chapter on him in Dr T. R. Glover's book, *The Conflict of Religions in the early Roman Empire*.

Born some time in the second century Tertullian was a native of Carthage. As a pagan he had been versed in the art of rhetoric and followed the calling of an advocate. He was a married man. Converted in middle life he took Orders, and wrote a number of works in the closing years of the century. Early in the third century he joined the movement known as Montanism. This movement is the first instance of what one may call revivalistic Christianity. Montanus, its founder, lived in Phrygia, and is a rather nebulous person. He seems to have taught that the second coming of Christ was to be expected, at a definite place in Phrygia and at an early date. He and some of his companions, among whom two women are mentioned in particular, laid much stress on individual inspiration by the Holy Spirit, and developed what came to be known as the New Prophecy. Clashes with ecclesiastical authority in the persons of Bishops in Asia ensued. According to the learned third-century writer Hippolytus, the Montanists claimed that through the teachings and writings of the Montanist prophets 'they had learned more than from the law and the prophets and the Gospels'. The movement was strongly ascetic and, if Tertullian is representative of it, protested against the worldliness which it thought to be affecting the Church. On points of discipline it adopted what we should call a rigoristic position. Second marriages were condemned; for grave sins after baptism there could be no forgiveness in this world. This whole point of view was thoroughly congenial to the fiery and uncompromising spirit of Tertullian. He threw in his lot with the New Prophecy which was now definitely a sect out of communion with the Church, and his connexion with the Church ceased. The date of his death is uncertain, but it may have been as late as the 'thirties' of the third century.

Tertullian, then, was a very different person from Irenaeus, but his influence upon Christian theology was as far-reaching, and, if we are thinking of terminology—of the best way of saying things,—more profound. To this his adhesion to Montanism made no difference. Montanism was not an intellectual movement at all. The breach between it and the Church did not turn on points of theology. And though there are respects in which Tertullian's theology is open to criticism from the standpoint of later orthodoxy, that has nothing to do with his Montanist views.

His own positions were worked out in the stress of controversy. As a controversialist he stands by himself in the history of the early Church. At this point we are concerned only with his writings against the Gnostics, of which the longest is his work against Marcion. Of another controversy of great importance, in connexion with the doctrine of the Trinity, something will be said in the next chapter.

Tertullian objects to the Gnostic doctrines on three grounds. First, they were suspect in origin. He thinks he can show that some of the most distinctive ones came from the philosophical schools of the Greeks. He was himself considerably indebted to Stoicism for some of his views, but he was no friend of the philosophers. He was less liberal in outlook than Justin had been—less liberal than his learned contemporary, Clement of Alexandria. But Tertullian was right in his underlying assumption that Christianity on its doctrinal side was not a product of any philosophical school. Secondly, the Gnostics had no valid authority for the doctrines which they taught. This is the argument of one of his early writings before he became a Montanist, the work *On Prescription*. Tertullian takes as the title a legal term which suggests that his opponents' case can be ruled out of court. He will not allow that they have any right to appeal to the Scriptures, since the Scriptures do not belong to them but to Churches which can trace themselves back to Apostolic founders.

'It is plain', he says, 'that every doctrine which agrees with those apostolic Churches, from which the faith had its birth and origin, is to be accounted as truth since it contains without doubt what the Churches received from the Apostles, the Apostles from Christ, and Christ from God; but that all other doctrine must be immediately accounted false, since its teaching is against the truth of the Churches and of the Apostles and Christ and God.'

Thirdly, the Gnostic assertions as to a supposed higher God than the Creator and their denials of Christ's true humanity were radically incompatible with the Christian Gospel. Marcion surrendered the fundamental truth that there is one and only one God, for Marcion did not deny that the Creator was God; only he said that there was yet another and a greater God. And the school of Gnostics which took its name from the teacher Valentinus surrendered the doctrine of the Incarnation, when they held that Christ was not of Mary, that as a spiritual being He merely passed through her and did not take from her the reality of human nature. For Tertullian saw clearly that such teaching, with its professed spiritual superiority, evacuated the Gospel of its supreme glory which was to be found in its faith in the Son of God as having truly been born and suffered and risen again.

So, with the help of such men as Irenaeus and Tertullian, the Christian Church emerged from the Gnostic controversy, unshaken in the substance of its faith, and more fully equipped on the intellectual side for the examination of other problems in theology which were demanding attention.

CHAPTER V

Difficult Questions and Attempts to Answer them

We have seen how the Gnostic assault upon the purity of the Christian faith was turned back. The Christian Church would not allow that faith to be transformed into an amalgam of Oriental ideas. In particular, there could be no compromise where the truths of the unity of God and of the reality of Christ's human nature were threatened. So there was firm insistence on the fact that the creation of the world was not the work of an inferior and even ignorant divinity, and that Christ did truly suffer in the flesh. The whole point of view which would allow to God no contact with matter either in creation or in redemption was definitely repudiated.

But there was no final settlement of all theological questions. About the end of the second century and well into the third century questions arose with regard to the doctrines of God and of the Person of Christ which were as keenly debated as any of the matters which had held the field in connexion with Gnosticism. They were of the first importance not only for that age, but for the whole later history of Christian thought. In a very real sense they remain vital issues on which decisions affecting the character of Christian theology have to be taken.

The problem centred in the fundamental belief in the unity of God. That was a fixed principle. Christianity was monotheistic religion. It recognized one

God only, not two or three or many Gods. How then was this to be held, and, at the same time, a Trinity of Persons, Father, Son, and Holy Spirit, to be affirmed? How was the divinity of Jesus Christ to be acknowledged without hindrance to the confession that God was one? We have seen that Justin was conscious of the problem. The way in which he speaks points to difficulties which he felt. And with all Irenaeus' firm grasp of the truths involved in the Christian Gospel about God and about Jesus Christ it cannot be said that he provides what could be called a solution, or attempt at solution, of the difficulties. It is different with Tertullian, and to him I shall come later.

Now we have noted the great use which the Apologists made of the idea of the Logos, of that divine Reason of God, who became incarnate as Jesus Christ. This idea had great value, but there were possible drawbacks connected with its employment. For when it was held that the Logos became personal and became Son of God when it was God's will to create the world through the agency of the Logos, it was too easy to think of the Logos as an intermediary between God and creation. Philo, the Alexandrine Jew, who took over the idea of the Logos from Greek philosophy, had thought in this way, and his notion of the Logos suffered from considerable obscurity; in his system the Logos is not fully divine. In the theology of the Apologists there is at times an approach to similarly unsatisfactory conceptions. A great German historian of doctrine described their Logos-doctrine as the doctrine of a 'depotentiated God', that is, of a God who lacks the full reality of Godhead. Such a description

74

does make plain the kind of difficulty which beset the Apologists and their failure adequately to extricate themselves from it. It was not so serious in the case of Irenaeus because in his theology the Logos doctrine is balanced by his emphasis on the divine Sonship.

But there were some who were content neither with the emphasis on the idea of the Logos nor with the kind of theology of which Irenaeus is representative. They were not satisfied that the doctrine that there is only one God was adequately safeguarded, and they looked for some other way whereby this could be achieved. So we come to the movement which is often described by the general title Monarchianism, because those who favoured it insisted that what they were concerned for was the 'monarchy' of God, that is, for the sovereign rule of the one God. This movement took two forms, of which the first was on the whole less important and certainly less philosophical. In this form the doctrine that there is one God was maintained by the denial of the divinity of Christ. Of the early representatives of this theology there is a very spirited account in a long fragment preserved by the historian Eusebius in the twenty-eighth chapter of his fifth book. He does not say who the writer of the fragment was; but he may have been Hippolytus, a theologian of great ability who had a rather stormy career in connexion with the Church in Rome in the early third century. The writer was certainly well acquainted with events at Rome. For the first champion of this Monarchianism was a Roman Christian called Theodotus, a leather seller, and he was excommunicated by the Roman Bishop Victor before the end of the second century. Theodotus gathered disciples round him, including another Theodotus, who was a financier; they made an attempt to found a Church of their own and even managed to get someone made a Bishop. We are not told how he was consecrated, and later he forsook the Theodoti and their friends and was received back into the Roman Church. Hippolytus, if it was he, says that the elder Theodotus was the first person to assert that Christ was a mere man. And as against this doctrine and its reaffirmation later by a certain Artemon, Hippolytus points out that it cannot be reconciled with the earlier teaching of the Church. He is especially indignant at the claim which Artemon and his friends made 'that the men of primitive times and the Apostles themselves received and taught these things as they are now taught by them'. They further claimed 'that the truth of the Gospel was preserved until the times of Victor, who was the thirteenth Bishop of Rome from Peter, but that from the time of his successor Zephyrinus the truth had been counterfeited'. Hippolytus counters this claim by a reference to writers of former days. 'I speak', he says, 'of Justin and Miltiades and Tatian and Clement and many others, by all of whom the divinity of Christ is acknowledged. For who does not know the works of Irenaeus and Melito and the rest, in which Christ is proclaimed as God and man?' He goes on to speak of the excommunication of Theodotus by Victor.

The teaching of Theodotus, Artemon, and their associates needs to be examined a little more carefully. The doctrine that Christ was a mere man was not the whole of their teaching about Him, and it is probable that they would have objected to the adjective 'mere' as giving a false impression of their views. What they seem to have held was that Jesus was a man miraculously born, in whom the Spirit dwelt to an exceptional degree, so that by the perfection of His life He attained to a state of unity with God which was equivalent to an ethical divinity. Thus the unity of Jesus with God was a unity of will. They gave no place in their doctrine to the thought of the preexistence of a divine Logos or Son of God who afterwards became incarnate. Thus there was no difficulty for them in upholding the unity of God. There was one God, and Jesus Christ was not the eternal Son of God, but, at most, a man who might be said to have been deified. And a deified man does not, as an idea, prove satisfactory to the thinking mind. For if a man could in very truth become God there would be a complete end to monotheism, and polytheism to any degree would become possible. Therefore we must say that in this theology the unity of God is preserved at the cost of the abandonment of the divinity of Jesus Christ. And that the Christian Church was not prepared to do. It held *both* that there was one God *and* that Jesus Christ was God. It held that truth was not to be gained by the abandonment of either of these doctrines, for both were true. This type of doctrine, sometimes called dynamic Monarchianism because it explained the personality of Jesus in part at least by its idea of the indwelling in Him of divine power, made no great headway. But we find it appearing again in the East much later in the third century under circumstances of special interest. In the year A.D. 260 a certain Paul, known from his place of

77

origin as Paul of Samosata, became Bishop of the important Church of Antioch in Syria. He was a man of ability, high in favour with Queen Zenobia, who for a time was an independent monarch in the East owing no submission to Rome. Under her Paul seems to have become a kind of finance minister, and to have combined for the first time in Church history the rôles of a statesman and an ecclesiastic. If the charges brought against him in a letter drawn up by a number of Bishops are trustworthy, he behaved at times in ways unworthy of the high ecclesiastical position he occupied. It is said that he reproved and insulted those who did not applaud the addresses which he gave in Church, that he extorted money for his personal use, and that, to quote from the letter in question, 'he stopped the psalms that were sung in honour of our Lord Jesus Christ, as the late compositions of modern men, but in honour of himself he had prepared women to sing at the great festival in the midst of the Church, hymns which one might shudder to hear'. How far these accusations were brought against Paul at the Councils of Bishops which were held to examine the doctrine which he taught we are not told by Eusebius, who gives us a good deal of information about the whole affair. He was accused of entertaining 'low and degrading views of Christ, contrary to the doctrine of the Church', and of teaching that Christ was in nature but an ordinary man; further, that he would not confess that the Son of God had descended from heaven, but said that Jesus was from below, that is, that He possessed no divine nature. His case ended in an interesting way. He was obviously skilful in argument and defended his views with ability, for it was not till two or possibly three Councils of Bishops had been held that Paul's views were condemned, and he himself deposed from the bishopric of Antioch. Another Bishop was chosen in his place. But Paul would not give way, and the sentence of deposition could not be made effective, since he had the support of Queen Zenobia who had the control of Antioch. However, in the year A.D. 272, three or four years after the final council, the Roman Emperor Aurelian defeated the forces of Zenobia, and her kingdom came to an end. An appeal was then made by the opponents of Paul to Aurelian, who for the greater part of his reign showed no tendency to persecute the Christian Church. Was Paul of Samosata in rightful possession of Church property at Antioch? That was the question. Aurelian decided that the property was to be given to whoever was recognized as the rightful Bishop by the Christian Bishops of Italy and Rome. This was the first legal intervention of the State in the temporal affairs of the Christian Church, and it resulted in the downfall of Paul. His doctrine seems to have been practically equivalent to that of the Theodoti and Artemon. But he was an abler thinker than they: as far as we know they had not introduced the Logos doctrine at all. Paul of Samosata taught that the Logos existed in God as His immanent reason, but was never to be regarded as personal. The Logos dwelt in Jesus as an inspiring power, and Jesus by moral effort, with the help of the divine power in Him, did become one with God in will and disposition. Thus Athanasius, writing in the fourth century, condemned Paul's views because they involved the notion that Christ became God after having been a man.

There has been much research during the present century into the character of Paul's doctrine, and competent scholars are not all at one in their conclusions. But at least it is clear that Paul laid the emphasis upon the human nature of Christ, and that the doctrine of Christ's preexistent divine Sonship was either wholly absent from his teaching or present in a way that sharply distinguished his theology from that of the Church. In his stress upon Christ's humanity Paul was typical of the general tendency of theologians connected with Antioch. One may say in general that the theologians of Alexandria emphasized the divinity of Christ and the theologians of Antioch His humanity. Each school was subject to a characteristic danger from the standpoint of the central faith of the Church. In that faith Christ was confessed to be both divine and human. At Alexandria there was, at times, a danger lest in the attention given to Christ's divinity His human nature should be emptied of its full reality; at Antioch the stress upon the fact that Christ was truly man could imperil the firm hold upon the belief that He, the historic Person who was born and died, had preexisted as the Son of God, and, at the Incarnation, had taken human nature. In the fourth and fifth centuries these divergent tendencies led to those controversies which resulted in the decisions of the third and fourth General Councils at Ephesus and at Chalcedon with regard to the unity of Christ's Person and to the reality both of His divinity and of His humanity.

In the form of the Monarchian doctrine which we have been considering the faith in One God led a number of people to deny the divinity of Christ. The other branch of Monarchianism took quite a different line. In its earliest, and one must say its crudest, representatives it taught that there was only one God, and that that God was Jesus. There was a certain Noëtus who lived in Asia Minor, and who expressed his belief in the words 'I know but one God: no other than He who was born, suffered and died'. According to Hippolytus he also said that the Father became His own Son. Then there was one Praxeas, who was the cause of one of Tertullian's most important treatises, called *Against Praxeas*. At the very beginning of the treatise Tertullian sums up his case against Praxeas in one of his most characteristic epigrams. Praxeas had come to Rome from Asia, and, according to Tertullian, had poisoned the mind of the Roman Bishop against the adherents to Montanism; he had also taught the same kind of doctrine as that we have observed in the case of Noëtus. 'So', says Tertullian, 'Praxeas did two pieces of work for the devil at Rome; he drove out prophecy and brought in heresy; he put to flight the Holy Spirit and crucified the Father.'

One may wonder how such doctrine could enter into anybody's head. For it clearly makes nonsense of the Gospels in which the Father and Jesus are two Persons, not one, and it involves the conclusion which may be expressed in this pictorial way that when Jesus Christ was on earth there was no God in heaven. And everyone, I imagine, would agree that no rational defence is possible of teaching such as this. But one can see the problem with which they were wrestling: how to affirm both the unity of God and the real divinity of Jesus. To say that the Father was the same as the Son was absurd, but it was also contrary to the first article of the Christian faith to say that the Father and the Son were two Gods. And to find the right way of expressing the truths to which justice needed to be done was not easy. It is not surprising that over and above the crudities of Noëtus and Praxeas we hear of unsatisfactory attempts at a synthesis. By far the most important of those who tried to work up this kind of Monarchianism into a philosophical theology was an Egyptian called Sabellius, who taught at Rome in the early third century. It is his doctrine which explains the adjective 'modalistic' sometimes given to this branch of the Monarchian movement. The word 'modalistic' implies in this context that Jesus Christ is God because He is one particular mode of the one God's self-manifestation. Sabellius taught that God revealed Himself in three phases, or three different rôles. Choosing the Greek word *prosopon*, which could mean 'person' but could also mean a mask, and therefore the part which an actor takes in a drama, he said that God revealed Himself in three successive prosopa, first as Father, then as Son, then as Holy Spirit. This was certainly a much profounder theory than those of the earlier thinkers on these lines, and Sabellius was remembered and his system spoken of long after theirs were forgotten. For this is an attempt to maintain a doctrine of the Trinity which safeguards the unity of God and does not identify, as Noëtus and Praxeas had done, the Persons of the Father and the Son. (It does not appear that they paid attention to the Holy Spirit.)

The objections to Sabellianism are both theological and philosophical. The theological objection consists in the fact that it cannot be reconciled with the New Testament which does not conceive of Father, Son, and Spirit as successive, but as simultaneous. They can be named together, and functions can be ascribed to them which differ in certain respects; but such functions can exist together. The philosophical objection consists in this, that, despite the Sabellian emphasis upon revelation, God is never really revealed. He is known only as playing a particular part. When the opponents of this system referred to Sabellius' doctrine as being that of a 'change-coat God' they were not really unfair to him. But perhaps because Sabellianism did really try to meet difficulties which confronted Christian thought it exercised a good deal of influence, and anything at all suggestive of it was viewed with the greatest suspicion in the East during the fourth century. Sabellius himself was excommunicated at Rome by the Roman Bishop Callistus, who himself did not find it easy to arrive at a satisfactory statement. According to Hippolytus Callistus went so far as to say that the Father suffered with the Son. As to such a statement, obviously a great deal depends on the meaning it was intended to convey, and one must remember that Hippolytus was a bitter enemy of Callistus, and may not have represented his teaching quite fairly.

We must now return to Tertullian and especially to his treatise against Praxeas. There is no single

Christian document between the New Testament and the Council of Nicaea in A.D. 325 which is so important in its bearing upon the future of Christian theology, and especially as providing a terminology which has maintained its place from Tertullian's time to our own. I do not mean to imply that this terminology has not been criticized. It has been and is. And, in any case, the thing which finally matters is not the adequacy or inadequacy of the form of words, but the truth or untruth of the ideas which the words are intended to express. But terminology is important. Ideas can never exercise their full force until they are clothed in suitable words, and until that verbal clothing is provided a cloud of obscurity will always hang over the ideas. And what Tertullian did was to frame a terminology which fitted theological ideas. He wished to express as clearly as possible the true doctrine about God and about the Person of Christ. And in doing this he was remarkably successful. There were elements in his doctrine which would be regarded as unsatisfactory from the standpoint of Christian orthodoxy; in this he differs from his great contemporary Irenaeus. Tertullian, despite his contempt for pagan philosophy, had a speculative strain in him such as Irenaeus never showed. And it is in some of his more speculative ideas that the defects of his theology lie. But these ideas, whatever be thought of them, do not affect his terminology at all. It is possible to correct or abandon the ideas and retain his terminology in full. Indeed, people who have never heard Tertullian's name use words when they are discussing the doctrine of God or of Christ which can be traced directly back to this

North African Christian. And to make that immediately clear I will anticipate what will come later in the course of this description and point out that one of those words is the word 'person'.

Let us start with the beginning of Tertullian's doctrine. God existed before all things, the one Reality. And yet, though the one Reality, God was not solitary for He always had reason within Himself. Tertullian preferred to translate the Greek word Logos as meaning reason rather than word, since reason precedes word which is the revelation of reason. Yet he admits that word as well as reason was always within God, since thought implies word. So he says of God that 'He has within Him reason even in silence, and in reason word'. Moreover, though this reason is immanent within God, in some sense the reason may be looked upon as another self. So as to the Logos who was always with God—one thinks of the first verse of St John's Gospel—he says, 'He who was is one, and He with whom He was is another'. Thus, even before the creation of the world there is more than undifferentiated unity in the Godhead. The next point in Tertullian's doctrine is related to the creation of the world. Up till then it could not be said that there was a Son of God. In another treatise, against one of the Gnostics, Tertullian says quite definitely 'There was a time when God had not a Son'. But now the Word is begotten: He proceeds from God to effect God's purpose of creation. And now it is possible to think of God as Father. Between the Father and the Son the closest unity exists: they are one thing in respect of unity of substance, though not numerically. The Son is God in virtue of the unity of substance. The word 'substance' is one which has passed out of use to a considerable extent in our time, especially in the language of philosophy. If we paraphrase it by some such form of words as 'real and essential being' we shall not be far off Tertullian's meaning. When he says that the Son is of the same substance as the Father, or, again, 'I do not derive the Son from any other source than from the substance of the Father', what he has in mind is the fact that the supreme reality which we call Godhead is the same in the Son as in the Father. At the same time, even in this respect Tertullian makes a distinction: he speaks of the Father as the whole substance and the Son as derived from the whole and a portion thereof. And, using a metaphor which played a considerable part in Christian thought, he described the Son as the stream from the spring, the ray from the sun. And then further, God the Unity does not evolve only a second distinct personal being but, to give Tertullian's own words, 'the Unity evolves a Trinity out of itself', and the Third is the Spirit who comes from God and the Son of God. The metaphor is continued. The Spirit is the river derived from stream and spring, the peak of the ray which proceeds from the ray and the sun.

So Tertullian reaches the completion of his doctrine of the Trinity. Starting from the Unity of the Godhead he would claim that he had maintained that Unity throughout. Affirming the distinction of the Three Persons, the Father, the Son and the Holy Spirit, he would deny that he had thereby introduced a doctrine of three Gods. For as to that which belonged to the unchangeable reality of Godhead, as to its substance, as to its power, there was no difference between the Three Persons; the difference appeared only in the relation of the Persons to each other, in the mode of Their existence, and in special characteristics. He expressly calls Each of the Persons Deus—God. He emphasizes the inseparability of Father, Son and Holy Spirit. As against those who insisted on the monarchy of God, the unity of the divine government, he urges that a monarchy is not endangered, is not less a monarchy, if it is administered, not directly by the monarch but by intermediaries. For if the divine rule can be mediated through angels, as the Scripture says, why, he asks, 'should God seem to suffer division and separation in the case of the Son and Holy Spirit who have obtained the second and third places as sharers in the substance of the Father, when no such division is the result of so great a company of angels?' And as a kind of summing up, Tertullian affirms that 'the monarchy resides in as many persons as God has willed'.

Tertullian reaches his conclusions by thinking of the Godhead, the divine nature, as one substance which is held by Three Persons. It is possible but not certain that his legal training helped him here, and that the idea of substance is helped out by the fact that, in law, substance could mean a piece of property, which could obviously be held in more names than one. In any case, it is to Tertullian that we owe the terminology of the one substance and the Three Persons, though it is worth noting that he uses the word 'Persons' very sparingly and prefers to speak simply of the 'Three'.

But the epoch-making value of Tertullian's language ought not to be allowed to conceal what must, I think, judged from any point of view, be regarded as defective elements in his thought. One might judge that his language implied that God was essentially and eternally the Trinity. As a matter of fact his thought is less satisfactory than his language. The Unity develops into a Trinity. God wills to be a Trinity. But Tertullian has not overcome the distinction between nature and will, and he speaks as though the Trinity were a fact resulting from the divine will rather than inherent in the divine nature. Moreover, he is not clear on the continuance of the Three Persons. Finally, when the administration of the divine government is given back by the Son to the Father, the distinction of the Persons will cease. How far this is really Tertullian's meaning is not certain, but if this is a correct interpretation of him, he is involved in the same inadequacy as besets the theology of Sabellius. The Son and the Spirit are temporary personal manifestations of God. Moreover, he seems to see a necessary element of the finite in the Son as compared with the Father: the Father is by nature impassible; the Son can suffer. Praxeas, against whom Tertullian wrote, held that the One God Himself could become finite and suffer; and a great German historian of doctrine has said that all this finitude and passibility Tertullian transfers to the Son. We must, I think, allow that while Tertullian's language is not only entirely compatible with the idea of an essential, eternal, Trinity, and, indeed, directly points that way, his thought comes short of that. Explanations which he gives and reservations which he makes suggest that he thought of the Trinity as a Trinity of manifestation or revelation.

In connexion with his doctrine of the Person of the incarnate Christ, his language was almost equally important. He thinks of Christ as possessing two substances, human and divine. Afterwards it became usual to speak of the two natures of Christ, but that does not represent Tertullian correctly, since for him nature is a quality existing in substance. Of these two substances there was a union, not a mingling, in Christ who is one Person, God and Man. In virtue of this reality both of Godhead and of Manhood in Christ, Christ could do those things which are appropriate to God, and suffer those things which are appropriate to man. Christ was one Person, the divine Logos incarnate. But because He had taken human nature (I use the more common term, rather than substance) He could, through that human nature, have experiences which would not have been possible to Him had He had only one nature, and that a divine one.

The controversies and the theology with which I have been dealing have their difficult sides. What I have tried to do is to make the main issues and the main results plain. And we have more than an academic interest in arguments and positions which contributed so much to the form in which the doctrines of the Trinity and of the Incarnation were stated and accepted in the Christian Church.

CHAPTER VI

The Christian Philosophy of Alexandria

There is a tradition that the Christian Gospel was preached in the great cosmopolitan city of Alexandria by St Mark the Evangelist. However that may be, Christians must have come to Alexandria and a congregation been formed there at an early date.

The great city had long been a centre of intellectual activity. The largest library of the ancient world was to be found there. All the chief subjects of learned study could be pursued at Alexandria under the guidance of competent professors. Jews were to be found in considerable numbers, and in Alexandria the Hebrew Scriptures were first translated into Greek. It was impossible for Jewish scholars not to be influenced by the Greek thought with which they were in so close contact, and, as a result, there arose what is called the Jewish-Alexandrian philosophy. Of this the most famous representative is Philo who was born about 20 B.C.

At Alexandria Christian teachers could not but devote much attention to the intellectual side of religion. Moreover, the Gnostic movement flourished in the city, and some of the great Gnostic leaders, such as Basilides, had their schools there. Persons who began to be interested in the Christian message were likely to ask in what relation Christianity stood to other forms of religious and philosophical thought. Nowhere was it more important that Christians should be able to give an answer concerning the faith which they held and the questions which arose in connexion with it.

It was, presumably, to supply that answer that there arose at Alexandria in the second century, for purposes of instruction, the institution which is known as the Christian Catechetical School. It seems to have been the result of individual effort rather than to have been definitely organized by the Christian Church in Alexandria. It is probable that it was viewed with some suspicion by certain of the members of the Church, and that they regarded it as inclined to over-emphasize the element of knowledge as compared with faith. This feeling cannot be ignored in connexion with the breach between Origen, the greatest of the teachers of the Catechetical School, and the Alexandrine Bishop Demetrius. With the special circumstances of that breach we shall not be concerned. But it is worth while remembering that the Christian philosophers of Alexandria resembled what today we should call a school of thought in the Church. They were not quite typical of the Church as a whole. A very close modern parallel would be found in the Cambridge Platonists of the seventeenth century. They revived some characteristic elements in the teaching of the Alexandrine theologians and resembled neither the High Churchmen nor the Puritans of Stuart times.

Of the first Head of the Catechetical School, Pantaenus, we know hardly anything. He is said to have been trained in the Stoic philosophy, and to have been not only a great teacher, but also a great missionary, and to have travelled as far as India. In any case, it was from him that Clement of Alexandria received that instruction in Christian doctrine which entirely satisfied his enquiring and, indeed, naturally restless mind. And towards the end of the second century this Clement succeeded Pantaenus as Head of the Catechetical School. There he taught till in the year A.D. 202 he left Alexandria during the great persecution which was then taking place. He went to Jerusalem, and it is clear that his action in leaving Alexandria was not regarded as unworthy. Alexander, Bishop of Jerusalem, could write of him later in terms of high approval, and Alexander himself in a time of persecution had suffered for Christ. But any tendency to rush upon martyrdom was disapproved by the wisest minds in the Church. Circumstances altered cases, and for some Christians it was a duty to follow quite literally a saying of the Lord in the Gospel: 'When they persecute you in one city flee ye to another'.

Clement was a man of great and varied learning. We possess a number of his writings, and though we cannot say that they give us a systematic philosophy or theology, they enable us to discern the main lines of his thought. He was deeply in love with the notion of truth, and it was as the true philosophy that Christianity specially commended itself to him. Here he wears the mantle of the Apologists, particularly of Justin. He was deeply impressed with the unity of truth: 'The way of truth', he says, 'is one, and into it as a never-failing river flow the streams on either side'. For him, Christ as the divine Logos incarnate brings to mankind that full light of which all earlier gleams had held the promise. In Christ all truth is unified. As he looks back over the ages of past human history he sees a process of preparation for Christ. Just as the law had been given to the Jews, so to the Greeks philosophy had been given to lead them to Christ. In one of his works the Logos is viewed as leading men onwards from imperfection and error, in another the Logos is the Tutor who builds up the character of the disciple. And in a fine passage from the seventh book of his longest extant work, the *Stromateis* or *Miscellanies*, he says of the Logos or Son of God that 'He is the Saviour, not of some only and not of others, but according to each man's fitness, He distributed His benevolence to Greeks and to barbarians, to faithful and elect persons, fore-ordained from among them and called at their proper season'.

In Clement, more than in any other Christian thinker, we see the union of the Greek philosopher and the Christian believer. He in whom the union of philosophy and faith is perfected is the true Christian Gnostic. Clement refused to surrender the word 'Gnostic' to those teachers who, while claiming the title, had transformed and, indeed, travestied the Gospel. Yet in his exalting of knowledge above simple faith Clement has some kinship with the Gnostic leaders. Faith is indeed sufficient for salvation, and is the necessary foundation of knowledge. But faith itself is simply the 'compendious knowledge of essentials', and above it stands the perfect knowledge, which cannot be obtained apart from philosophy. On this Clement is quite definite: he expresses it in this way: 'Whosoever would attain to knowledge without philosophy, dialectic, and the study of nature is like him who expects to gather grapes without cultivating the vine'.

Clement's debt to Greek philosophy is apparent in connexion with his thought about God: indeed in his doctrine there is certainly a tension and, it might be true to say, an actual conflict, between ideas derived from Greek metaphysics and ideas directly connected with the Old Testament and with the teaching of Christ. On the one hand God is utterly transcendent, pure Being, that which is. He is describable only by negatives, by saying what He is not. Thus, to speak of Him as the One is really to go too far, for God is beyond unity. Properly speaking, neither qualities nor relationships can be ascribed to Him. The names given to Him are of value in supplying the correct lines of thought about God, but that is the extent of their value. This is the language of what is sometimes called the *via negativa* or negative way of knowing God, whereby men may understand what God is not. Parallels could be adduced from Plato and Philo. Carried to an extreme, which is just the logical conclusion of his method of approach, it is quite incompatible with the Christian doctrine of the Incarnation, for this involves the belief that in Christ there is a true revelation of what God is. Otherwise such texts as 'It is God that hath shined in our hearts to give the light of the knowledge of the glory of God in the face of Jesus Christ', and 'He that hath seen me hath seen the Father', would be entirely meaningless. These texts may be taken as illustrations of the fundamental Christian conviction that the word 'God' does not stand for a metaphysical abstraction but for the Father of our Lord Jesus Christ, the Father who has manifested Himself in the Son. And because Clement was a Christian he could not be content to speak simply in the language of non-Christian philosophy. On the contrary, he can speak as the simplest of believers would speak of the goodness and friendliness and providence and pity of God. He knows that God desires the salvation of men. He sees the proof of God's nature in the Son who comes as, in Clement's words, 'a certain activity of the Father'.

Clement, as I have suggested, continues the tradition of the Apologists in connexion with the Logos doctrine. He insists that God was never without the Logos, who is His Son. It is possible that he thought of the Son as of one substance or being with the Father. He speaks of the Logos as the beginning and first fruits of the things which exist, being Himself timeless and without beginning. The Logos is the countenance of the Father, and in Him the Father is known. Apart from the Logos the Father cannot be known as He is, nor described, but is the object of faith alone.

Clement was something of an intellectualist. He belongs to the class of people who exist both within and outside of Christianity and believe that mankind needs to be taught rather than to be healed. So he lays stress on the teaching given by Christ, the Logos incarnate. Knowledge was one of the supreme gifts which Christ came to bring. So, Clement says, the Logos was made man that we might learn from man how man may become divine. It is interesting to note in Clement the influence of the Gnostic tendency to make little of the reality of Christ's human nature. Clement can say that Christ did not need to eat or to drink, except for the purpose of refuting those who should deny that He was truly man. Such an argument is clearly self-destructive. If Christ's human nature did not, in and for itself, need the support of food it was a human nature essentially different from ours.

With all his learning, Clement was not a great constructive or systematic thinker. But he did two notable things: he showed more fully than anyone before his time that Christianity had the power to meet men's intellectual enquiries; and he was the teacher of Origen.

Origen is one of the most extraordinary men in the history of the Christian Church. So many sided is he, so dramatic in the character of his life, so encyclopaedic in the range of his learning, so comprehensive in the subjects of his writings, so profound and so daring in the quality of his thought, that his place is among the select few of the first class. Yet as compared with many thinkers, Christians and non-Christians, incomparably his inferiors, he is little known. Here I can do no more than attempt to give some impression of the man and of his work. He was born in the year A.D. 185. His parents were Christians of good position in Alexandria. His father was put to death in the great persecution in Egypt in A.D. 202–3, and the youthful Origen might have shared the same fate had not his mother resorted to the simple but effective device of hiding his clothes, 'to compel him', as Eusebius the historian, a great admirer of Origen, says, 'to remain at home'. To his father in prison he wrote: 'Take heed not to change thy mind on account of us'. When Clement left Alexandria, Origen, while only in his eighteenth year, succeeded him as chief Christian teacher at Alexandria. He combined wide learning and assiduous study with a life of the most severe and ascetic character. He had at first the confidence and support of his Bishop, Demetrius. He gave much attention to Greek philosophy and defended himself when attacked on the ground that he devoted too much time to it. His defence is worth quoting: 'When people came to visit me, some from heretical sects, and some who were conversant with Greek studies and especially with philosophy, I thought it well to enquire into the doctrines of the heretics and into those works of the philosophers which claim to speak of truth'. He argued that he was but following the example of Pantaenus 'who before our time helped many', and of his own associate Heraclas, who was a priest of the Church in Alexandria and wore the philosopher's cloak. Origen did not confine himself to Alexandria. Different causes took him to Rome, to Arabia, to Palestine. It was in Palestine that the first clash with Bishop Demetrius occurred. Origen, though still a layman, was requested by the Palestinian Bishops to expound the Scriptures in church at Caesarea. Demetrius, when he heard, remonstrated. The Palestinian Bishops defended themselves by quoting various precedents of which they knew. Demetrius recalled Origen to Alexandria, and there he resumed his work. His output was immense, especially in the way of Commentaries on books of the Old and New Testaments. And before he left Alexandria, not to return, he had completed the great work *On First Principles*, which may be regarded as the first Christian systematic theology ever composed. Unfortunately, for a great part of it, we are dependent upon a Latin translation. A wealthy friend provided him with seven writers to whom he dictated. They, so Eusebius tells us, relieved each other at appointed times. The 'labour-loving' Origen, as Athanasius was to call him, needed, or, at least, took, but little rest. In the year A.D. 230 came the decisive break with Bishop Demetrius. Origen, passing through Palestine on the way to Greece, was ordained priest by the Palestinian Bishops. Demetrius was very angry, not unnaturally, for it could fairly be claimed that the question of Origen's admission to the priesthood lay with the Bishop of the Church in Alexandria. And it was now that Demetrius brought up in condemnation Origen's act of literal interpretation of Christ's word in the twelfth verse of the nineteenth chapter of St Matthew's Gospel. Origen settled in Caesarea. A local Council of Bishops and Presbyters at Alexandria went so far as to excommunicate him, but of this decision there was nothing like general acceptance. He continued his teaching and literary work, was invited to Arabia to take part in an important doctrinal discussion, and finally encountered in his own person, during the persecution set on foot by the Emperor Decius in A.D. 250, those sufferings which he had wished to undergo nearly half a century earlier. He was not actually put to death, but the tortures he endured must have been the cause of his death.

Any account, however brief, of Origen should start with his life, for we ought not to lose sight of the heroic man in the erudite scholar and theologian. And whatever faults there were in Origen's life, however much we may feel that he did not always act in a wise or well-balanced way, it cannot be denied that no man ever sought to serve the cause of sacred learning, which for him was the cause of Christ, more ardently, wholeheartedly, and sacrificially than Origen.

And now let us look at the theologian. Origen was Clement's pupil and successor, and owed much to him. And like Clement he desired to represent Christianity as the true knowledge. Yet between the two men there are not unimportant differences. Origen had studied Greek philosophy and made use of various ideas to be found in the philosophical systems, but he set less store by philosophy than Clement had done. His starting-point was the revelation given in the Scriptures and the truth of the Church's tradition. He followed out the rule which he laid down in the preface to the great work *On First Principles* that the successors of the Apostles were to build up their scientific system on the basis of the given articles of faith. At the same time, in Origen as in Clement, we may see Greek ideas and influence present in his conception of God. And the resulting difficulties which we have noted in the case of Clement make their presence felt in Origen. He emphasizes God's transcendence. God cannot properly be described as Mind or Essence since every description falls short of Him. Once again we meet with this negative way of the knowledge of God. It is possible to say what God is not, not what God is. But with abstractions of this kind Origen could no more be content than could Clement or any Christian. God for him is no impersonal being or force, but personal, self-conscious, loving. On God's activity as Creator he laid great stress. God must create as fire must shine. Time and matter alike owe their existence to Him. Yet Origen did not think of the world as created in time; he thought of an eternal act or process of creation. This is a point where Origen diverges from what has been commonly held among Christians. It is important to realize that Origen did not intend to ascribe to matter or to the world any kind of existence independent of God. Origen does not believe in two original principles—God *and* the world—but in God as the eternal Creator, whose Almighty power is thus eternally displayed.

This doctrine of God becomes clearer through Origen's doctrine of the Logos or Son of God. It has been said that Origen was always anxious to refute two views; the first is any confusion of the person of the Son with the person of the Father, such as was involved in the teaching of Noëtus and even of Sabellius. A German scholar puts it in this way: 'Origen regarded it as a truth certain above all else that the Son could only be a being personally distinct from the Father and self-subsisting'. The other view, which Origen always challenged, was that which would separate the divine nature of the Son from that of the Father. In respect of divine nature, of Godhead, the Father and the Son were one. There is a passage in Origen's commentary on the Epistle to the Hebrews which can only mean that Origen taught that the Son was of one substance or essence with the Father. In it is found the very Greek word *Homoousios*, meaning 'of one substance or essence with', which was given so important a place in the Nicene Creed at the Nicene Council of A.D. 325, and stands in that fuller form of the Creed which is recited today. Thus Origen taught the eternal, personal, existence of the Son of God, and repudiated any idea of there ever having been a moment when He did not exist. And here we come across Origen's special contribution to the doctrine of God. Some earlier thinkers, influenced by the idea of Logos as meaning immanent reason, had tended to think of the Logos as not at first Son of God. The Logos became Son through an act of God which is described, after human analogy, as generation or begetting. So the Logos becomes personally distinct as Son. Origen went deeper. Whether with implicit criticism of former views or because the notion of a divine Sonship which yet was not eternal seemed to him impossible, he formulated the idea of the eternal generation of the Son of God. 'As is the brightness from light,' he says, 'so is that eternal and everlasting generation,' and again, 'The Saviour is ever being begotten by the Father'. Thus the relation Father-Son is interpreted by Origen as an eternal relation within the Godhead. So he maintained the true Godhead of the Son, and at the same time gave the one satisfactory answer to Sabellius. God had not, as Sabellius had taught, manifested Himself first as Father, then as Son, but the distinction between Father and Son was a real and eternal distinction.

At the same time, Origen had not cleared up all difficulties, and the student of Origen becomes aware of another side to his thought. This side is at times so prominent that Origen seems to be taking away with one hand what he had given with the other. And in later ages, long after Origen's death, sayings of his were recalled which seemed to imply that he was the forerunner of Arius and of the doctrine that the Son of God was a creature, though the highest of creatures. Then Origen's name was held not in honour but in execration. A brief statement of the causes which gave rise to this view of Origen will help us to understand some of the difficulties which confronted a philosophical theologian who was trying to do justice to the many-sidedness of truth as he saw it.

Origen's conception of the transcendence of God was derived on its metaphysical side from Plato and the later Jewish-Alexandrine thought of Philo. In this thought much was made of the need for a mediating agent between God and the created world, in order that God might not be conceived of as in direct contact with matter. This partially explains the prominence given to the Logos in Philo's system. It is obvious that such a mediating agent will be regarded as less than divine. Now Origen, partially at least, accepts this standpoint. He thinks of God as creating not directly but through the Son; there is an immediate relation of the Son but not of the Father to the created world. In a curious passage he speaks of the Son as having a place in a series leading downwards from God to the heavenly bodies, which bodies he regarded as semi-divine beings, a view of the stars not uncommon in the ancient world. Moreover, Origen thought it necessary to emphasize the dependence of the Son upon the Father. With his strong insistence upon the distinction

of the Son from the Father there went an emphasis
upon what was involved in the priority of the Father.
He did not think of this priority as one of time, but he
did hold that a difference was to be noted in the fact
that the Father alone was the Fountain of Godhead,
the absolute principle of being. Thus, when Origen
thinks of God as the supreme Cause of all that is he
tends to think of the Father. He can even speak of the
Son as the most ancient of all the works of God, when
he is thinking in terms of what philosophers would call
the principle or category of causality. And Origen
also felt bound to give an explanation of such passages
of Scripture as those in the Gospels in which Jesus
says 'Why callest thou me good; none is good save
One, that is God', and again 'My Father is greater
than I'.

Great scholars have differed in their interpretations
of Origen. Everyone would agree that he said things
which a century later would have been impossible for
anyone who desired to be regarded as in line with the
Nicene Creed. But if that is taken to mean that Origen
was really an Arian before Arius I must express my
dissent. What Origen makes plain is the difficulty
which could arise when the Christian doctrine of God
was expressed by means of philosophical ideas which
were in themselves non-Christian:—I do not say anti-
Christian. Origen did not believe the Son of God to be
only partially divine; it was the fulness of Deity which
the Son possessed from the Father, and of the Father
He was the perfect and eternal mirror. But if, as some
philosophical systems suggested, the essence of Godhead was to be found in sheer underived existence, in

the idea of God as the Absolute, to use a later philosophical term, then the Father alone could be regarded in this light. Later theologians may have condemned Origen, but not the great Athanasius in the heat of the Arian controversy. He knew there were things in Origen to which exception could be taken, but he did not hesitate to quote him as on his side in that controversy, and I believe he was right in doing so.

The perplexities which beset the student of Origen's doctrine of the Son of God extend in the same sort of way to his doctrine of the Holy Spirit, and therefore of the Trinity. One has to recognize the existence of more than one strain of thought. And to the doctrine of the Holy Spirit not nearly so much attention had been given. So in Origen we meet with statements which imply the true and eternal divinity of the Holy Spirit, and with others which emphasize the subordination of the Holy Spirit as compared with the Father and the Logos. Yet in general we may say that Origen did much to help towards a more scientific statement of the doctrine of the Trinity. And the doctrine itself he took not from philosophy but from Scripture and the Creed.

When Origen came to frame his doctrine of the Incarnation he was influenced by his belief in the pre-existence of souls. He held that the divine Logos united Himself with the one soul which had remained pure and faultless. This soul was the intermediary between the Logos and the physical body. So Origen laid great stress on the human soul in Christ, and it is worth while remembering that the doctrine of Christ's true and complete humanity on which the Christian

Church has insisted involves the recognition of the fact that Christ possessed a truly human soul.

Further into Origen's theology I cannot enter here. Where he felt himself free to do so, he speculated boldly, and it would not be true to say that his speculations have met with wide acceptance. He taught a doctrine of many super-material worlds, of the pre-existence of all souls in those worlds, where all except one sinned, of atonement as a ransom paid by Christ to the devil. This curious view was by no means peculiar to Origen and indeed was widely accepted until Anselm, the great Archbishop of Canterbury in the early twelfth century, gave it its death blow. Origen also taught the final disappearance of all evil, and that all men and all spiritual beings would eventually be saved. Whatever we may think of such views, and however we may judge of the value of the characteristic contributions of Origen to Christian theology, we shall at least feel that here was a man who tried to rise to the height of a great task, the task of seeing existence steadily and as a whole.

CHAPTER VII

Scripture, Creed, and Church

The progress of Christian theology owed very much to the work of particular men. Such contributions as those made by Irenaeus, Tertullian, and Origen were of the highest importance. But one would give a very false picture of the state of things in the early Church if one concentrated attention simply on the labours of distinguished theologians. In order to understand those labours, and the spirit and standpoint of the thinkers in question, one must appreciate the context of Christian thought and life in which they had their place. For that context was the permanent background of the writings of individual thinkers, and by its stability exercised a controlling influence. Moreover, it involved a theology which represented the common faith of Christians, not the speculations of particular teachers. It is this context or environment that we now need to consider; and our attention may be given, first of all, to the formation of what is called the Canon of the New Testament, that is, of a recognized library of sacred and authoritative books in addition to those already existing in what we call the Old Testament.

I pointed out in an earlier chapter that the writers of the books which comprise our New Testament had no idea of adding a second volume to the Old Testament. Each writer had a particular object in view when he compiled his book. The evangelists wished to tell the story of Jesus, the author of the Book of Acts to show how the primitive Church began to grow, and how the Christian good news was preached in important cities of the Roman Empire. St Paul wrote to Galatia to prevent the Christians there, his own converts, from falling back into the observance of rites and ceremonies of the Mosaic Law. St James' Epistle was motived by the author's desire to emphasize the necessity for a lofty moral standard: and so on. But it was certain that these writings would be valued in a rather different way by the Christian communities which received them. It is worth while remembering that these books were not at once known throughout the whole body of Christian believers everywhere. Whatever circulation of such writings went on, some of them must for a time have been in the possession of particular Christian communities. And the community would set high store on the book or letter it possessed. It would tend to regard it not simply as supplying information about the life of Jesus, if the writing was a Gospel, or as dealing with specific questions affecting the welfare of the community, if it was an Epistle, but as a guide in matters of Christian faith and Christian conduct. In other words, the community would look on the book as one that had authority. One can easily see how that would happen. The Gospels were full of sayings of the Lord Jesus. The great German scholar who died recently, Adolf von Harnack, has said with regard to the motives that led to the creation of the New Testament that 'the earliest motive force, one that had been at work from the beginning of the Apostolic Age, was the supreme reverence in which the words and teaching of Christ Jesus were held'. Moreover, the validity and power of the Christian appeal depended not simply, one may even say not most profoundly, on the sayings of Jesus but on the history and personal significance of Jesus, on what He had done and what He was. Especially was this important when it was necessary to engage in controversy, whether with Jews or with Gentiles. The Gospels which met this need were as important for Christians as the Mosaic writings (I take the common title and raise no questions of authorship) were for Jews. And as the Mosaic writings had long been considered sacred and authoritative writings in Judaism, it was not surprising, rather was it inevitable, that Christians would regard as sacred and authoritative those Gospels which were concerned with One who was in their estimation infinitely greater than Moses. It did not matter that Jesus had not Himself written the Gospels, as it was believed that Moses had written the Pentateuch. It was sufficient that they were written by men qualified to do so. Again, the Epistles came with the authority of Apostles or of men closely associated with Apostles. This was especially the case with the Epistles of St Paul, which gained a place in the collection of sacred writings from the earliest time when the idea of a New Testament Canon began to take shape. And the proof of the recognition of a particular book as sacred and authoritative was the fact that it was read in the public services of the Church.

But the Canon of the New Testament was not formed all at once, even when the idea of a further volume of sacred books began to lay hold on the Church; yet one fact was of great importance in hastening the process. The controversy with the Gnostics in the second century reacted on the whole question of authority in religion. How were the claims of the Gnostic sects to be met? One of the ways was by challenging their right to represent themselves as the exponents of the truth of the original Gospel. For the Gnostic leaders contended not only for the intellectual superiority of their teachings but also for the truth of those teachings as grounded in apostolic traditions and writings. So there arose the necessity of distinguishing between writings and especially Gospels which were genuine, the work of Apostles or of apostolic men, and writings which were forgeries put together in order to support some set of Gnostic doctrines and circulated under the name of an apostle of Christ.

I think many people would both appreciate our New Testament more and realize something of the motives which led to its compilation as a body of sacred writings, if they had some acquaintance with that collection of documents which is known, as a whole, as the Apocryphal New Testament. The whole of this literature can now be obtained in a single volume, translated by Dr M. R. James, Provost of Eton, and published by the Clarendon Press, Oxford. It is a volume of some five hundred and fifty pages, and contains translations of apocryphal Gospels, Acts, Epistles, and Apocalypses. The word 'apocryphal' is probably known to most of us through its association in our English version of the Old Testament with a number of books like Wisdom and Ecclesiasticus, which form as it were a little volume of their own. They were not part of the Jewish Old Testament which consisted of books written in Hebrew. 'Apocryphal' does not, primarily, mean spurious, but hidden or secret. And, to quote Dr James, 'Such books were almost always issued under venerable names, which they had no true right to bear. . .the pretence was that these had lately been brought to light, after ages of concealment by pious disciples'. Thus the transition to the idea of apocryphal as meaning spurious or false was not difficult. The apocryphal literature of the New Testament is by no means all of a piece: much of it has no connexion with the Gnostics, but the appearance of works claiming an authority to which they had no real title, and the association of a few of these works very definitely with the Gnostics, made the question of sacred and authoritative books a vital one in the second century. And by the end of the second century the New Testament, as a collection of books, had taken shape. We possess a very important fragment of about the year A.D. 170 written at Rome and dealing with the New Testament as the author knew it. He recognizes the four Gospels, the Acts, all St Paul's Epistles as we possess them, the Epistle of St Jude, two Epistles of St John and one of St Peter, and the Apocalypse of St John. He does not mention Hebrews or the Epistle of St James. He probably says (the text is uncertain at this point) that there was a second Epistle of St Peter 'which some of our friends will not have read in the Church'. And he makes no reference to a third Epistle of St John. This testimony gives us the New Testament as accepted in

Rome near the end of the second century. Broadly speaking it agrees with evidence we have from other parts of the Christian world, from France for instance, in the writings of Irenaeus, and from Africa in those of Tertullian. But it was a long time before there was universal agreement. In different parts of the Church there was a disinclination to include some work which stands in our New Testament—now it was Hebrews, now the Epistle of St James, now the Apocalypse: or, perhaps, there was an inclination to regard as canonical some book which does not stand in our New Testament, for instance *The Epistle of Barnabas* or *The Shepherd of Hermas*. And it is noteworthy that the great Athanasius, Archbishop of Alexandria, is the first person to lay down the twenty-seven books of our New Testament as alone canonical. This he does in an Easter Letter which he wrote in the year A.D. 367. This date may be regarded as marking the end of the period of uncertainty. As a matter of fact, with regard to by far its largest part, there was a common mind in the Church as to what constituted the New Testament two hundred years earlier.

I hope that this brief survey of some of the relevant facts connected with the New Testament in the primitive Church will have made two things clear: first, that it became at a comparatively early date essential that the Christian communities should come to decisions with regard to the books to which appeal could be made concerning the character and content of Christian doctrine; secondly, that there was no single decision which constituted the Canon of the New Testament: we must realize that a process of selection was going on. But the importance of the recognition of an authority of the books was very great, especially as what we call Bible-reading was very common in the early Church. The Christian layman with a Gospel or an Epistle in his hand was in a strong position for resisting open attacks upon the Christian faith, or the more subtle attempts to change its character which were made by the Gnostics.

Another fact of great significance, as providing a standard for the layman's thought and the theologian's interpretation of doctrine, was the rise, certainly in the West, of a definite creed. I say certainly in the West, because, while we are able to trace the growth of the Creed in different parts of Western Christendom, there is much less evidence as to what was taking place in the East, and the evidence which we have points less surely to one conclusion.

For the beginning of Creeds we must go back beyond the New Testament to the Old. There, in the sixth chapter of Deuteronomy, we have a fundamental statement of Jewish faith in the unity of God: 'Hear, O Israel: the Lord our God is one Lord': and the command to love God with the whole heart and soul and strength was the proof of the Creed's value for life. It had a meaning for the whole man, not simply for his intellect. Now, when we come to the New Testament, this belief in the unity of God remains fully in possession. But that was not the *distinctive* belief of the early Christians. That distinctive belief is to be found in the two Greek words Κύριος Ἰησοῦς, Jesus is Lord. How much was involved in this simple but profound testimony to Jesus two passages in St Paul's Epistles

make plain, the third verse of the twelfth chapter of
1 Corinthians where the Apostle tells his readers that
'no man can say, Jesus is Lord, but in the Holy Spirit',
and the ninth verse of the tenth chapter of Romans, 'if
thou shalt confess with thy mouth Jesus as Lord, and
shalt believe in thy heart that God raised him from
the dead, thou shalt be saved'. And while I do not
believe that we can find in or extract from the New
Testament a formal creed consisting of a number of
articles there are passages which show the beginnings
of that process. Thus, in the sixth chapter of Romans,
St Paul speaks of Christians as having obeyed a form
of teaching to which they had been delivered—his
characteristic way of putting what we should more
conventionally describe as the teaching delivered to
them. In the Pastoral Epistles—the two to Timothy
and one to Titus—there are passages which suggest
that form or terminology was becoming more fixed as
when in the second chapter of the Second Epistle to
Timothy we read of a 'pattern of sound words'. Moreover, the association of God or the Father, and the
Lord Jesus, and the Holy Spirit, as in the baptismal
formula at the end of St Matthew's Gospel, or in the
very familiar passage with which 2 Corinthians ends—
The Grace of our Lord Jesus Christ, the love of God,
the fellowship of the Holy Spirit—and in other places,
may rightly be taken as preparing the way for a Creed
in which there should be three main divisions.

The question whether, theoretically, a definite and
authorized Creed is a good thing—in Christianity or
in religion generally—is hardly relevant here. So far
as primitive Christianity is concerned it is a very

academical question. For it was inevitable that the content of Christian faith should be made plain. There was very little merely conventional Christianity in the first and second centuries. It is true that not all the members of the Church were examples of Christian conduct, but the position of a Christian in the world at that time was a difficult one, and at any moment might become dangerous. Both for the sake of those who wished to join the Christian society and for the sake of the society itself it was necessary that there should be no misunderstandings as to the faith which membership involved. Moreover, there were teachers—the Gnostics—who claimed that the true Christian faith could be discovered only through attention to their doctrines. It was not a time when the vagueness as to the substance of Christian faith could be regarded as a virtue.

As to the date when a Creed composed of a number of articles first existed, there is no exact agreement, nor have we precise knowledge of the facts attending its compilation. But one may say with confidence that round about the middle of the second century there existed at Rome a Creed which we have only to read in order to recognize in it the earliest form of that Creed which today we call the Apostles' Creed. This Creed in substantially the same form was known by Irenaeus in South France near the end of the second century, and by Tertullian in North Africa at the beginning of the third. It came to be used, sometimes with slight changes, in other Italian Churches besides Rome—I may mention Milan and Ravenna. Finally, as a result of developments which took centuries to complete, the full form of the Creed as it is known and used today came into existence.

That is a very brief statement dealing with a subject which has given rise to so much discussion. For our knowledge of the early history of Creeds has resulted from the industrious researches and trained acumen of scholars who have worked over the wide fields of Christian literature from the beginning of the second century onwards. And while there are still some un-settled questions, we shall scarcely include among them the original form of the Creed: it ran, as nearly as possible, as follows:

> I believe in God the Father Almighty;
> And in Christ Jesus, His only Son, our Lord,
> Born of the Holy Spirit and Mary the Virgin,
> Under Pontius Pilate crucified and buried,
> On the third day He rose again from the dead,
> He ascended into the heavens,
> He sat at the right hand of the Father,
> Whence He cometh to judge living and dead.
> And in the Holy Spirit,
> Holy Church,
> Forgiveness of sins,
> Resurrection of the flesh.

This Creed, which was spoken of as the symbol, or the rule of faith, was taught to those who were being pre-pared for Christian baptism. At the actual time of baptism, which probably took place on Easter Eve, it was put to the candidate in a shortened, interrogative form, and the candidate, in reply, made profession of his faith.

With regard to the Creed itself, a number of points deserve comment. In the first place, no attempt is made either to find a place for all Christian beliefs or to give theological explanations of what is included. The Creed is not a philosophy, but a statement of essential Christian conviction centred in the faith in Jesus Christ as the Son of God. Secondly, the form of the Creed may have been influenced by the need for excluding those misinterpretations of Christian belief which were common in the Gnostic schools. Our conclusion as to this will depend partly on the date that we assign to the Creed. The Gnostic teacher Marcion was in Rome, and, for a time, a member of the Roman Church, shortly before the middle of the second century. It has been suggested that the Creed arose in protest against his doctrines and that we can see in the text of the Creed signs of a definite intention of controverting that doctrine. But the majority of scholars date the Creed earlier than Marcion's arrival in Rome. If he found himself able to accept it at first as Christian truth, in the course of a few years he developed his own teaching in such a way that he found himself in sharp opposition to some of the articles of the Creed, and was expelled from the Church. What is probably the case as to the origin of the Creed is that while it was framed in a positive and uncontroversial way before the Gnostic controversy became acute, it did act as a necessary and most valuable barrier against the kind of re-writing of Christian doctrine which Marcion and other Gnostics attempted. For instance, the Creed gives no ground for the distinction between the true God and the Creator on which Marcion laid such stress. It is implicit in the opening sentences of the Creed that there is one God, who is the Creator of the world and also the Father of the Lord Jesus Christ. It is true that the words 'Maker of heaven and earth' did not find their way into the Creed till a much later date, but the word 'almighty' was sufficient by itself to indicate the true relation of God to the world, especially when taken with the word 'Father'. For while in early Christian literature God was constantly thought of as the Father of Christ, He was also thought of as the Father, that is, the Creator and Governor of the world. Again, the view of Christ's human nature as illusion and of the Crucifixion as mere appearance which some Gnostics held, was quite incompatible with the Creed, which asserts quite positively the birth, death, and burial of Jesus the Son of God. Further, the Gnostic tendency to make a sharp distinction between spirit and body, and to represent the body, and, indeed, matter as a whole, as valueless if not actually evil, is sharply checked by the final article of the Creed in which the resurrection of the flesh is asserted. It is not surprising that there are many Christians today who feel a very real difficulty about this phrase. The phrase 'resurrection of the *body*' which came into use in England in the sixteenth century would generally be regarded as preferable, while the clause at the end of the Nicene Creed, 'I look for the resurrection of the dead', has still fewer disadvantages. To go into questions concerning the Christian doctrine of immortality would be beyond the scope of this book. But it is certain that, from the first, Christian belief has involved the idea of resurrection and not simply the Greek notion of the immortality of the soul. Emphasis is often, and rightly, laid on the fact that St Paul's argument in the fifteenth chapter of 1 Corinthians rules out materialistic conceptions of resurrection. But there can be no doubt at all that with regard both to Christ and to Christians St Paul taught a doctrine of resurrection. If he had been contending simply for a belief that man has a soul which survives bodily death, his argument would have taken a completely different form. What I think we may see both in St Paul's teaching and in the earliest form of the Creed is the conviction that the whole man, body and soul, is the object of God's redeeming love and becomes a sharer in the Kingdom of God.

A Christian of the second or third century was fortified in his faith by the books of the New Testament which bore witness to the teaching and the work of the Lord Jesus and of the Apostles, and also by the Creed which marked off the elements of true belief from doctrines which could make no good claim to be part of the original Gospel. There was one more support to which he could turn, the support of the Church, the Christian society, the true People of God to which he belonged. There has been, and is, abundance of controversy concerning the nature of the Church: but it is not a controversial statement if I say that the history of early Christian life and thought cannot be understood unless attention is paid to the prominence given to the idea of the Church. That prominence grew out of the belief that the Christian people, as a religious society, inherited the privileges and promises once granted and made to the people of Israel. So the Christian society was the true Israel. It was also, in the words of one of the most remarkable phrases ever coined by St Paul, the body of Christ. Such language implied and fostered an immensely strong sense of unity and continuity. It did not mean simply an emphasis on what today is sometimes contemptuously called institutional religion, but stood for the reality of religious fellowship recognizable by certain definite signs. That was part, at least, of the importance attaching to the Christian ministry and the Christian sacraments. Through them, as through the sacred books and the Creed, Christian believers were welded together into a unity. It was impossible for Christians who believed that the Church was a holy society, which existed in the midst of a hostile or indifferent world to bear witness to Christ, to be indifferent to religious unity. One of the charges brought against the Gnostics was that they developed their teachings apart from the Church. They had no credentials to show which could substantiate their claims. There was no true line of continuity linking them with the Church of the Apostles. A different kind of controversy arose at Carthage in the middle of the third century. After the terrible persecution set on foot by the Emperor Decius the question arose as to whether those who had in one way or another denied the faith during the persecution could ever be received back into membership of the Church. There were some who denied that this was possible. They took up the position which Tertullian had adopted in his Montanist days, that persons guilty of certain grave sins could never be restored to Church fellowship. They failed to convince the majority of their fellow-Christians in North Africa; in particular,

SCRIPTURE, CREED, AND CHURCH

the great Bishop of Carthage, Cyprian, refused to
adopt this rigid view. A schism resulted, and the ad-
vocates of unflinching sternness towards those who had
fallen away during persecution organized themselves
into a separate community. A great theological question was at the centre of this problem of discipline. Did
the holiness of the Church mean that gross sinners were
to be permanently excluded? Or was there hope of
restoration even for them? The character of Christianity as a religion of redemption in which there was
no limit to God's grace and to His willingness to for-
give was at stake. Had the rigid view prevailed the
Church would have shrunk to a society of the morally
respectable; the sheep that had never strayed would
have had its permanent place in the fold, but there
would have been no return for the sheep that had
wandered into the wilderness. It is not, I think, surprising that one of the greatest of third-century
Bishops, Dionysius of Alexandria, accused Novatian,
the protagonist of the rigorous view, of 'slandering
our most compassionate Lord Jesus Christ'.

Controversy of this kind must not lead us to read
back into the third century those discussions and differences about the Church and about its ministry and
Sacraments with which we are familiar. Those discussions belong, on the whole, to a later age. The
Christian of this early age saw in the ministry of the
Church, and especially in the Bishops, the guardians
of Christian truth and the dispensers of those sacraments which were at once pledges and channels of the
grace of God. Anything like a merely symbolic view
of the sacraments was certainly alien to Christian

120

thought. For the emphasis was laid upon what man received from God in the sacraments, not on the sacraments as signs of man's faith.

During the third century Councils of Bishops for the settlement of questions, sometimes of doctrine but more frequently of discipline, began to be held with increasing frequency. But as yet these were local councils, consisting of Bishops who dwelt in particular areas. No council intended to be representative of the Bishops of the whole Church had yet been held. But that was soon to come; and my last topic will be the great Council held at Nicaea in Asia Minor in A.D. 325. It was called together as a Council of the whole Church, it issued a Creed for the whole Church, and the main subject of its deliberations was the true doctrine concerning the Head of the Church, the Lord Jesus Christ.

CHAPTER VIII

The Council of Nicaea

The first decade of the fourth century witnessed the final attempt of the pagan Roman Empire to crush the Christian Church. The Emperor Diocletian had made great constitutional changes; he had divided the Empire into an Eastern and a Western section. He was the supreme ruler in the East, the Augustus, and he made an old comrade in arms, Maximian, the ruler, the Augustus, in the West. To each Augustus was attached a subordinate ruler, who bore the title of Caesar.

It was not till some twenty years after Diocletian's accession in A.D. 284 that he set on foot the last and greatest of the persecutions. To this day his motives are obscure. Others, and especially Galerius, the Eastern Caesar, were probably more violently opposed to Christianity. Diocletian may have thought that the progress of Christianity threatened the well-being of the Empire by leading to a neglect of the old gods under whom Rome had grown great. Whatever the causes and motives, the persecution was violent and sustained; in the East especially there were scenes of terror of which Eusebius has left us a record. But it was impossible to carry the policy through to victory. Not all who were responsible for putting Diocletian's edicts into effect were prepared to co-operate wholeheartedly. Gradually the persecution diminished. And then the need for a change of policy became plain. That change may be summed up in one word, *Toleration.*

The Empire recognized that the destruction of the Christian Church was beyond its power. True statesmanship realized that only one course was open, to give to the Church the sanction of the Law's approval. Edicts of toleration were issued in A.D. 311 and again in A.D. 313. The long drama that had lasted for two and a half centuries was at an end. Finally, as a result of political changes and military movements into which I need not enter, the Empire was once more united under a single ruler. His name was Constantine. Not till he was on his death-bed in the year A.D. 337 was he admitted by baptism to the Christian Church, but for a quarter of a century before that he regarded himself as a Christian. He told the historian Eusebius, the Bishop of Caesarea, that on one of his military expeditions he had seen a vision of the Cross in the sky. There has been much controversy as to his character, as to the motives of his religious policy, and as to the results of that policy. But one thing is certain, Constantine, of definite conviction, turned his back upon the pagan Empire and set his face towards a Christian Empire. Rightly is he spoken of as the first Christian Emperor.

The Empire needed peace and unity. For unity, wherever it could be achieved, Constantine was enthusiastic. He desired, and had done much to bring about, the cessation of religious strife, at least in its outward manifestations, as between Christian and non-Christian. Little did he dream that within the Christian Church the battle for unity on an issue of fundamental importance was about to be fought.

It was at Alexandria that the storm-cloud appeared.

There was a priest of the Church in Alexandria, one Arius, a man of distinguished appearance, with the capacity, as a teacher, of making his meaning quite clear. In the year A.D. 317 his doctrine began to make a stir. He was accused of saying that the Son of God was a creature, not eternal, not truly divine. The Bishop of Alexandria found it necessary to intervene. He was, indeed, personally involved, since Arius seems to have developed his own doctrine in reaction against what he regarded as Alexander's tendencies to Sabellianism. Sabellius had failed to distinguish adequately the Persons of the Father and of the Son. Alexander seemed to Arius to be making in the same direction. But if the Father was the one eternal Creator, and the Son simply the best and noblest of creatures, then any danger from Sabellianism was at an end. And this sheer difference between the Father and the Son was the truth—so Arius held and so he taught.

Alexander tried to settle the question on peaceful lines. He may have hoped to convince Arius both that he, Alexander, was not a Sabellian, and that Arius' teaching was unsound and inadmissible. He failed. Arius was not an easy person to shake. Finally, in the year A.D. 321, a Synod was held at Alexandria, and Arius was deposed from the office which he held as one of what we should call the parish priests of Alexandria. But that meant, not the abating of the storm but the letting out of more waters. Arius did not lack influential friends and supporters even among the Eastern Bishops. How many there were who really approved of Arius' own doctrine we do not know. I am not inclined to rate the number as a high one. But there were plenty of people who dreaded anything that could be represented as Sabellianism more than they dreaded anything else, and were not prepared to have a venerable presbyter like Arius sacrificed to a Bishop tarred with the Sabellian brush.

Meanwhile Alexander and his friends were not idle. Among them was a young Alexandrine cleric, Athanasius, the foremost of the deacons in the city and already of note for a brilliant piece of theological work, a dissertation entitled *On the Incarnation of the Logos*. He seems to have been responsible for the circulation to Christian Bishops in all parts of an account of what had taken place, and of the reasons for the deposition of Arius. And now the Emperor became fully aware of the sharp controversy which had burst out in the second city of the Empire, and of the likelihood of its extension. This was quite contrary to his mind. So he sent to Alexandria the Western Bishop whom he trusted most, Hosius, Bishop of Corduba in Spain. Hosius was to effect a reconciliation between Alexander and Arius, and restore peace. Constantine probably thought that there was simply a tiresome but trifling theological dispute which tact and good sense could bring to an end. He was to learn that one of those issues had arisen which refuse to be settled by any formula of compromise, since in the cause of truth men must answer either 'Yes' or 'No'. Hosius returned with his mission unfulfilled. The Emperor now decided to call a Council of Bishops representative of the whole Christian world. The Council met in the year A.D. 325 in the small town of Nicaea in the north of Asia Minor. There were other matters which came up for settlement, but everything was dominated by the doctrinal question.

There is something of an epic character about the Arian controversy and the Council of Nicaea. The story of the drama of the Council is told with extraordinary vividness by Dean Stanley in his book *Lectures on the History of the Eastern Church*. Not less vividly, and with profounder insight, has the course of the controversy been surveyed by Professor Gwatkin, who succeeded Creighton in the Chair of Ecclesiastical History at Cambridge, in his book *Studies in Arianism*. The Council was, in point of fact, mainly composed of Eastern Bishops; very few Western Bishops were present. But few who are conversant with the proceedings and results of the Council will challenge its right to be considered an Universal, that is, to use the technical term, an Oecumenical Council of the Church. Constantine himself opened its proceedings and exhorted the Bishops to be at unity among themselves; he seems now and then to have taken some part in the discussions.

The Council was a great assembly of Bishops, with the Bishop of Rome represented by two legates. Hosius of Corduba was there, and Eusebius of Caesarea, the great historian who has been called the Father of Church History, and another Eusebius, Bishop of Nicomedia, Arius' friend and ablest supporter. But no Bishop stands at the centre of the drama of Nicaea. That place is reserved for two men of inferior rank in the Church, who had no direct standing or voice in the deliberations of the Council, Arius the deposed priest and Athanasius the chief deacon of the Church in Alexandria. They represented, as no others did, the sharply contrasted positions. And before I go on to speak of the doings of the Council I will try to set forth those positions in their salient features.

Arius thought of God as existing alone in solitary majesty from all eternity. His nature was utterly transcendent and aloof. He lived alone, nothing existing except Himself till it was His will to create the world. But to create the whole world and all existences, spiritual and material alike, would be unworthy of God. So God brought into existence a being of incomparable excellence to be the agent through whom the work of creation should be accomplished. This being, the first and supreme creature, was called Son or Wisdom or Word. But he was not in any way the immanent reason of God; he was not one with God in nature, nor indeed was his nature like to the divine nature. The word 'begotten' used of him in Scripture did not, in Arius' interpretation of it, imply any kinship of nature or substance between him and God. This Son of God was, in fact, simply the highest of created beings. The 'perfect creature' is the phrase which Arius uses about him. Yet the word 'perfect' must not be misunderstood. Arius held that the Son of God, like any other creature, possessed free will and was not necessarily and unalterably good; that he had remained good was due to the right exercise of his own freedom and to God's grace. Moreover, the Son's knowledge of God was limited; Arius says 'the Word cannot perfectly and exactly see or know His own Father'.

Such then, in the theology of Arius, was the nature of the being called the Son of God, whom God created in order that through his instrumentality the world might be created. Though Arius was willing to bestow upon him exalted titles, even to speak of him as 'God' and to allow that worship might be paid to him, it is obvious that such a being possesses no rightful claim to divinity. This Son of God is not divine, and Jesus Christ, who is this Son of God become incarnate, is not divine. It is interesting to note that Arius taught that the Son or Logos had at the Incarnation taken to himself a human body, but not a human soul as well. There was no need in the Arian theology for the idea of a human soul in Christ, since the place of the soul was taken by the Logos, who, as a creature, could be subject to all those experiences which we associate with a human soul. We see in the theology of Arius the presence and influence of ideas with which we have already met. But Arius carried certain tendencies to their furthest conclusions. The Apologists in the second century had not reached a stable or satisfactory view of the Logos as the agent in the work of creation. There is too much of a suggestion that the Logos is intermediate between God and the world; but a creature He was not. He was the indwelling reason of God who is afterwards begotten as the Son. There are inadequacies and inconsistencies in the thought of Tertullian and of Origen, but neither of them is an Arian before Arius. Each may state the doctrine of the Trinity, or try to give a reasoned interpretation of the doctrine, in a manner which raises real difficulties. But no one can deny that Tertullian and Origen give us a doctrine of the Trinity, and that is precisely what one cannot affirm of Arius. A remote God, a created

Son who has no kinship of nature with His Creator, a yet more subordinate Holy Spirit—with such conceptions as these a credible doctrine of the Trinity cannot be constructed. Arius relied on certain Scriptural passages, such as the verses in the Book of Proverbs in which the author makes Wisdom say 'The Lord created me a beginning of His ways'; and the words in St John's Gospel, 'My Father is greater than I'. He argued that a Son must be later in time than a Father. He rejected Origen's idea of the eternal generation, apparently on the ground that it involved a materialistic conception of God, and involved the ascription to God of bodily passions. Origen, of course, had meant nothing in the remotest degree materialistic, but was simply trying to express by way of human analogy the truth of real, divine Sonship. For Arius there is no such thing as real, divine Sonship. 'The Son' is no more than the first of creatures.

I think that the best introduction to the theology of Athanasius may be found in some lines of Browning in his poem *Christmas Eve*, where he imagines an old German professor feeling the need for a more positive Creed than the critical theories which have formed the substance of his lectures. The poet continues:

> When thicker and thicker the darkness fills
> The world through his misty spectacles,
> And he looks for something more substantial
> Than a fable, myth or personification,—
> May Christ do for him what no mere man shall,
> And stand confessed as the God of salvation!

For Athanasius was not primarily interested, as Arius seems to have been, with the problem of creation, but with the problem of redemption, of the restoration of sinful man to fellowship with God. It was Athanasius' conviction that the key to that problem was to be ound in God's own will to bring man back to unity with Himself. This was the motive of the Incarnation; this was what Christ had accomplished. And this meant that Christ Himself was truly divine, true Son of God, not a supreme creature or demigod. 'He became Man', says Athanasius in the treatise *On the Incarnation*, 'that we might be made divine', that is, that human nature purified by His presence might recover the blessing of communion with God. Athanasius, deeply conscious, as many a man of religious insight has been conscious, of the gulf between God and man which moral evil has caused, was sure that a bridge across the gulf had been built by God's own action. God had visited and redeemed His people. Athanasius would have said, as the most influential of the Protestant theologians of Germany, Karl Barth, is saying today, that there is a road from man to God because, and only because, there is first of all a road from God to man. And both, in their own ways have said, 'that divine road is Christ'.

From this root-conviction that Christ is the true and therefore the divine Redeemer the theology of Athanasius develops. He was not a great speculative thinker, a master of philosophical technique. But he was wholly alive to the need for a theology that should express the heart of the Christian religion which is to be found in the sense of the infinite debt owed by the Christian to God, revealed and redeeming, in His Son Jesus Christ our Lord. And he was assured that any theology which failed to express the true Godhead of Christ came infinitely short of what was needed. So he contended, not for a word but for a vital, the vital, truth, when he insisted that Christ the Son of God was of one substance with the Father. I could not put Athanasius' doctrine of the Person of Christ better or more briefly than in the words used by Professor Gwatkin with regard to the essence of true Christian belief—that Christ is as divine as the Father and as human as ourselves. He who was the eternal Son of God took to Himself human nature. It is the doctrine of the Prologue to St John's Gospel: 'The Word was made flesh and dwelt among us'. And so, whereas Arius in his doctrine of God can find no place for any conception except that of a solitary personality, Athanasius, while he maintains as strongly the truth of the divine unity, conceives of the Father and Son as constituting a duality within the unity, and when the belief in the Holy Spirit is added the notion of the Trinity is complete. What we note in Athanasius is the real importance which he assigns to the ideas of divine Fatherhood and divine Sonship. For Arius, both terms, however much hallowed by traditional usage, were mere figures of speech. God created a being to whom the name of Son was given. Athanasius, while recognizing that Fatherhood and Sonship are terms borrowed from a human relationship, insisted that these human terms do express the true character of a divine relationship. The highest reality of Fatherhood and Sonship existed eternally within the Godhead; and Jesus Christ, the Word of God incarnate, was the everlasting Son of the Father.

9-2

The accounts which are given us by the Church historians enable us to gain a clear impression of the course of proceedings at Nicaea, even if we cannot attain to certainty on every point. Three parties may be distinguished at the beginning of the Council. There was a small group of convinced supporters of Arius, of whom the most notable was Eusebius, Bishop of Nicomedia. In sharpest opposition stood Alexander, Bishop of Alexandria, and some others, among whom may be mentioned Eustathius, Bishop of the great see of Antioch, Hosius, Bishop of Corduba, and the two priests who represented the Bishop of Rome. In between came the majority of the Council; adherents of Arius they were not, but the fear of anything which savoured of Sabellianism held them aloof from Alexander and his friends. They are sometimes spoken of as conservatives, a term which in this context would imply that, basing themselves on traditional lines of thought, they were averse from the imposition of any new formula, especially if it contained a technical term not found in Scripture. The most eminent of this large section of the Council was the other Eusebius, the historian, Bishop of Caesarea. It would appear that the first move was made by the Arian group. They put forward a Creed which was indignantly repudiated and torn up. The Council showed itself to be decisively opposed to the Arian doctrine. Then Eusebius of Caesarea intervened. He has left us a record of what took place in a letter which he wrote to his Church at Caesarea. His prestige was great; he was the trusted confidant of the Emperor; he sincerely desired to fulfil the office of a mediator and to ensure a conclusion satisfactory to all. So he came forward to present to the Council a Creed on which all might agree. It is not certain, but it is probable, that this Creed was in substance the Creed taught to candidates for baptism in the Church of Caesarea. Eusebius, not without reason, hoped that it would meet all needs. In this he was disappointed. Yet the reason is simple. This Creed, composed long before the Arian controversy had broken out, did not sound a decisive note on the point at issue. It could be interpreted in more ways than one; it did not specifically rule out the idea that the Son of God was Himself a creature. It was an admirable document for anyone who wished to avoid a clear-cut decision. There can, I think, be no doubt that the Arian group would have accepted it. Not so the friends of Alexander. They were determined to make it clear beyond question that the Church's faith in Christ was faith in one who was true God. We know from a work of Athanasius, in which he deals with the Council of Nicaea, how strongly he felt that he and his friends were not innovators, were not introducing a new doctrine. He goes back over the course of Church history to call in the evidence of great teachers of earlier times, among them Origen. Exactly how the decision was arrived at to make Eusebius' Creed the basis of a Creed set forth with the authority of the Council, but to strengthen it with phrases which should definitely exclude the belief of Arius and his supporters, we do not know. Eusebius says that the Emperor thoroughly approved the Creed which he had presented but desired the addition of the one word *Homoousios*, meaning that the Son is of one substance with the Father. Yet Constantine can hardly have suggested this addition unprompted. Moreover, it was far from being the case that Eusebius' Creed remained unchanged except for this one addition. Eusebius recognizes that the Creed actually composed and approved varied in other respects from his own, and does not seem to have been pleased with the fact. Much was done to leave no room for ambiguities. It is significant that even the word Logos which stood in Eusebius' Creed was omitted, perhaps because of unsatisfactory inferences which had been drawn in connexion with it. And not only was the Son described as of one substance (or being) with the Father, but also as from the substance (or being) of the Father, whereby the unity between the Father and the Son in respect of Godhead was yet more clearly emphasized. The three words, 'begotten, not made', which also did not stand in the Eusebian Creed, constituted another direct reply to the teaching of Arius. Whereas Arius held that the Son was a creature and that to speak of Him as begotten was only another way of saying that He had been created, the revised Creed put the two words in sharp contrast. Moreover, as the doctrine of the true Godhead of the Son was freed from any kind of ambiguity, so was the full reality of the human nature which He took at the incarnation affirmed by the two expressions which follow one another in the original Greek as two single words—'was made flesh, became man'. In the Eusebian Creed the phrase 'was made flesh and dwelt among men' could have been interpreted in the Arian sense that at the incarnation the Son took to Himself only a human body, not a human soul. In the revised Creed the true and full humanity of Christ is made as plain as His true and full divinity. The revised Creed ran as follows:

We believe in one God, the Father almighty, maker of all things both visible and invisible. And in one Lord Jesus Christ, the Son of God, begotten from the Father as only-begotten, God from God, that is from the substance of the Father, light from light, very God from very God, begotten not made, of one substance with the Father, by whom all things were made, both the things that are in heaven and the things that are on earth: who for us men and for our salvation came down and was incarnate, became man, suffered, and rose again the third day, ascended into heaven, and is coming to judge living and dead. And in the Holy Spirit.

To this positive expression of faith was added a rejection of a number of distinctive Arian tenets, for instance, of the views that the Son was not eternal, that He was created, that He was capable of changes. Those who hold such opinions 'the Catholic Church anathematizes'.

The two phrases, 'of the substance of the Father' and 'of one substance with the Father', call for special comment. In our understanding of them we may be handicapped in two ways. First, we may have gained the impression that the word 'substance' and the idea which it conveys belong to an antiquated philosophy. Secondly, 'substance' may suggest something material and, because of that, unworthy of association with God. The second difficulty may be cleared away at once; nothing materialistic was intended by those who secured the insertion of the word. Athanasius was not less convinced than Arius that God was pure Spirit. As to the former difficulty, it would largely be removed if we translated the Greek word by the phrase 'of one being with the Father', rather than by the words which stand in our English version of the Creed, 'of one substance with the Father'. Such a translation would do no injustice to the original Greek. For what the Greek phrase means, and what the other phrase 'of the substance (or being) of the Father' means, is that, in respect of fundamental nature, no distinction can be drawn between the Father and the Son. As the Father is truly God, so the Son is truly God. At the same time, the phrases do not imply that the Father and the Son are one Person, which would amount to an extreme form of Sabellianism. Undoubtedly, part of the objection to these phrases was bound up with the suspicion that they involved a Sabellian doctrine. But to say that the Son was of one being with the Father does not mean, and was not intended to mean, that the Son is the same Person as the Father.

The clear-sightedness and determination of the group with which Athanasius was associated prevailed. When the Creed came before the Council for signature all the Bishops signed except either two or five. That many signed not without misgivings the subsequent history suggests. That history goes beyond the period covered by this book; it is, in its way, a continuation of the Nicene drama, full of vicissitudes, full of attempts to substitute another Creed for that of Nicaea. Those attempts were often backed by imperial favour. But through the long years Athanasius, who had become Archbishop of Alexandria, stood firm. Driven into exile five times, even as after Nicaea Arius and those who did not accept the Creed were exiled, Athanasius never compromised. And when he died in A.D. 374 it was within seven years of the end of the long controversy. At Constantinople, in A.D. 381, in what is regarded as the Second General Council, the Nicene Creed was reaffirmed. And that Creed, though in a longer form, with the declaration that Christ is of one substance with the Father, remains the most universal Creed of Christendom.

It is a grave error to imagine that men fought so keenly for a word. It was the character of the Christian Religion which was at stake at Nicaea. For religion means, among other things, worship. In religion of the most primitive kind the element of worship had its place—no small one. Men of many views will be at one in holding that man's worship and adoration should be paid to no one less than God. To refuse to worship Christ would, long before the days of Athanasius, have outraged Christian feeling. But how to adore one who is no God but only the most excellent of creatures? For Athanasius, religion and theology must in so great a matter be at one. The theology of Christ's true Godhead, and nothing short of that, could answer to the demands of Christian faith and Christian religion. That too, was nothing new. Far back from New Testament times religion and theology had advanced together to this end. But at times the issues seemed confused, and illumination was only partial. With Athanasius and Nicaea all lesser controversies were merged in a conflict which went down to the foundations of Christian faith and experience. And where the battle was most directly joined there was fullness of light and clearness of vision. It was the light which comes at times to show that a tempting middle course is not the way of wisdom, but that it is the way of wisdom no less than the way of courage to give to a great question the answer 'Yes' or 'No'. To that wisdom and courage the Creed of Nicaea is an abiding testimony.

For EU product safety concerns, contact us at Calle de José Abascal, 56–1°, 28003 Madrid, Spain or eugpsr@cambridge.org.

 www.ingramcontent.com/pod-product-compliance
Ingram Content Group UK Ltd.
Pitfield, Milton Keynes, MK11 3LW, UK
UKHW012327130625
459647UK00009B/123